Antislavery Origins of the Civil War
in the United States

# Antislavery Origins of the Civil War in the United States

BY

DWIGHT LOWELL DUMOND

FOREWORD

by ARTHUR SCHLESINGER, JR.

THE UNIVERSITY OF MICHIGAN PRESS

*First edition as an Ann Arbor Paperback 1959*
*Second printing 1960*
*Copyright © by the University of Michigan 1939*
*Foreword copyright © by the University of Michigan 1959*

*Published in the United States of America by*
*the University of Michigan Press and simultaneously*
*in Toronto, Canada, by Ambassador Books, Ltd.*

*To*

IRENE MARGARET DUMOND

*Manufactured in the United States of America*

# FOREWORD

by ARTHUR SCHLESINGER, JR.

IT IS FITTING that this important work be republished on
the eve of the hundredth anniversary of the Civil War. There
is no more compact and incisive account available of the rise
of moral protest in America against the system by which one
human being owned another. Mr. Dumond describes graph-
ically how the awakening exasperation of the people at
last confronted the nation with the question it had dodged
since independence: whether an ostensibly free state, founded
on principles of liberty and equality, could tolerate in its
midst a system of human bondage. This was the terrible
contradiction in the heart of American society; and what Mr.
Dumond so well understands is what Abraham Lincoln meant
when he said, "Without the institution of slavery, and the
colored race as a basis, the war could not have an existence."
To sensible people looking back at the Civil War, Lincoln's
remark may not seem particularly arresting. But a generation
of 'revisionist' historians arose to reject the full implications
of the Lincoln thesis: this revisionism, which for a moment
held sway in the historical guild, ended almost by revising
slavery out of existence as a prime cause of our national
tragedy.

When the revisionist historians minimized the slavery question, they naturally had no choice but to see the war as a
needless conflict, brought about by a blundering generation.
By refusing to consider slavery a moral issue, they denied
themselves the ability to understand the emotions, north and
south, which forced the American Union to its moment of
truth. By thus draining the moral content out of history, they

reduced the Civil War to an ignoble and wanton affair, an episode of passion and demagogy. Mr. Dumond's book helps restore the moral dimension to our understanding of the war. He recognizes that the presence of a Negro minority (then as now) "has always provided the acid test of American democracy." He recognizes too the obligation of the historian to "recover the emotions which surge through men's hearts and alter civilizations." And his rebuke to the revisionist misunderstanding of Lincoln makes a distinction which should control historians as well as statesmen: "It is unfortunate that, because he did not hate slaveholders, historians should conclude that he did not hate slavery." The breadth of research, the cogency of presentation, the sensitivity of historical imagination and moral insight—all this make Mr. Dumond's book one of the neglected classics of our Civil War literature.

# CONTENTS

# ANTISLAVERY ORIGINS OF THE CIVIL WAR IN THE UNITED STATES

## I. THE UNFINISHED TASK OF THE FOUNDING FATHERS

THE war which raged in the United States from 1861 to 1865 remains, in many respects, the most interesting war in all history. Historians have never agreed whether it should be called a civil war, a war between the states, a rebellion, or a war for Southern independence. Nor do they agree which of its contributory causes should be most emphasized. Some say that war was forced upon the South as the final act in a crusade to abolish slavery. Others interpret it as a desperate struggle to check centralization of power in the federal government and to preserve the constitutional safeguards of minorities against majorities in the nation at large. A few strive, with indifferent success, to find its origins in the dissimilar economic development of the two sections.[1] An occasional reference is still made to secession as the achieve-

[1] It is my purpose in these lectures to trace the antislavery movement in broad outline from its origins to the Civil War. Economic issues were involved in the trend toward sectionalism. Rival economic groups used the slavery issue to their own particular advantage. The antislavery movement was not self-contained, nor did it exist independently of other phases of a general movement for social reform. Any attempt to deal with these broader aspects of the history of the period within the scope of eight lectures would detract from my main purpose. I do not believe, however, that the impulses back of the attack upon slavery and of its defense were economic. The antislavery movement was an intellectual and religious crusade for moral reform. The defense of slavery was of a social system and a system of racial adjustment, not of an economic institution.

ment of a well-organized conspiracy by disgruntled politicians.

It is not strange that there should be this lack of agreement. Social, economic, and political issues had combined through the years to array section against section in continuous strife, yet, even as the war began, there was no unanimity of opinion in either section on any of the questions in dispute. In the Confederacy men who owned no slaves, and never hoped to own any, fought side by side with great slaveholders who knew that the war, won or lost, would probably mean emancipation, perhaps servile insurrection and military despotism. In the Union men who hated slavery, but were unconcerned about political institutions, coöperated with men who repudiated abolition doctrines yet looked upon dismemberment of the Union as a greater calamity than loss of life itself. Resistance to centralization of power under President Lincoln by the followers of Clement L. Vallandigham was as bold and defiant as it was to the arbitrary acts of President Davis by the followers of William L. Yancey and Alexander H. Stephens. No one loved the Union more than John C. Calhoun or reverenced the Constitution more than Stephens. The Southerners were not dissatisfied with the Constitution, but rather with the antislavery interpretation of it. William Lloyd Garrison cursed it; they adopted it as their instrument of government.

Thirty years of intense intellectual ferment had failed to clarify the confusion of ideas and conflicting claims relative to (1) the capacity of the Negroes for intellectual and moral improvement; (2) the probable consequences of complete emancipation without their removal from the country; (3) the utility and character of the institution of slavery; (4) its status under the Constitution; and (5) the nature of the federal government, the limits of its powers, and the residuary authority of the states. Nevertheless, *majority* opinion in each of the two sections had tended to crystallize on opposite sides of these questions. Great principles of human rights and human relationships such as were involved in these questions cannot be compromised, though men may be prevailed upon to forego a test of armed strength for a time in hope that they will triumph in the ordinary course of events. In this instance marshaling of armaments did not occur until 1860, but hatred had smoldered in men's hearts three decades before, needing only the fierce winds of political revolution to fan the flames of civil war. Many men from both sections searched diligently for some formula by which to make the adjustment necessary for a harmonious and continuous existence as one people, but their statesmanship proved inadequate. A crisis was reached with the triumph of the Republican Party in 1860. Our search for the origins of the Civil War, therefore, will first require a brief outline of the steps by which the two sections of the country were brought into hostile array.

All historians are agreed that there would have been no civil war if there had been no American Negro slavery. He who would write the history of that conflict, then, must first recount the nature of a social malady so deep-seated that it ofttimes threatened the principles of civil rights forever associated with the nation's birth; sundered its churches and its political parties; reached into the sacred confines of man's oldest institution, the family, setting brother against brother and father against son in deadly combat; and, finally, severed the nation into two republics whose systems of government require the most careful scrutiny to be distinguished one from the other. Slavery, as it has been studied and revealed to us, would never have done those things. Slavery as revealed to the Northern people, not alone by the abolitionists, but by the course of events, did do them. We are forced, therefore, to the conclusion that the study of American Negro slavery has been inadequate; that, in its broader aspects, slavery was national rather than sectional; and that any pattern of it reconstructed from plantation life or from Southern documentary sources alone can be but fragmentary.

Scholars have too long focused their attention upon the Old South. Diligent search has been made for every sort of document surviving the ravages of war in that section which would throw light upon the nature of the civilization that was destroyed. Literature long available on the antislavery movement has been neglected, as well as a search for the voluminous but unrecovered private manuscripts which must, in the very nature of things, still be extant. It is my purpose not to attempt a complete reëvaluation of the institution of slavery, but rather to analyze the abolition indictment of slavery and to trace the steps by which the defense of the institution forced men to proceed from a generous discussion of the subject to a war against it.

Finally, there is the problem of how and why slavery became a political question of national import. The philosophies of the Constitutional Democrats and of the Republicans, constructed around the doctrines of the concurrent majority and the higher law, respectively, grew out of the early phases of the slavery controversy and developed with the trend toward sectionalism. The ultimate objectives of the proslavery forces and of the antislavery forces never changed; each advanced from one position to another in search of effective means by which to accomplish its purpose: complete emancipation on the one hand, absolute security for the institution on the other. Each step brought them nearer to the organization of a Southern sectional political party and a Northern sectional political party, each party seeking control of the federal government and each espousing constitutional interpretations and political theories which would enable it to fulfill its mission. On the day that those two parties presented their platforms and their candidates to the electorate sectionalism was complete, the question of slavery and the question of governmental structure were synchronized, and a dual revolution was in progress.

The history of the antislavery movement falls roughly into three periods. Events of the first period center around the activities of the American Colonization Society, an organization which drew its support from all sections of the country and from all classes of men—slaveholders and non-slaveholders, proslavery and antislavery advocates—who, for one reason or another, sought to expatriate the free Negro. It came to an end with the organization of the American Anti-Slavery Society in 1833, by which time the question of slavery had become almost entirely sectional. The second period extended from 1833 to 1839. During those six years lines for and against slavery were sharply drawn; a crisis was reached and passed in the struggle to prevent the philosophy of slavery from completely dominating the country; the fundamental principles of antislavery doctrine were clarified; the North was abolitionized and covered with a vast network of antislavery societies. The third period began with the adoption of the principle of direct political action by a portion of the abolitionists in 1839 and with the organization of the Liberty Party. We must, of necessity, sketch but briefly the main outline of events before 1833, and then turn our attention to the thirty years of organized antislavery effort.

Slavery had cast its dark shadow across the deliberations of the Constitutional Convention of 1787, threatening its disruption, raising doubts as to the ratification of the new instrument of government, and calling forth dire prophecies of future discord between sections. The founding fathers, either from fear of alienating the support of two or three states or from utter weariness of a long-sustained struggle for principles, or, as the abolitionists later contended, from the belief that slavery was a decadent institution destined to early extinction, left the question of its status under the Constitution indefinite. If one accepts the last view, then indeed do we have a perfect example of the inability of men to look at the seeds of time and determine which will grow and which will not grow. Every Northern state had abolished slavery before the closing of the foreign slave trade in 1808. No Southern state had done so. Virginia's delegates to the Constitutional Convention had raised their voices against continuation of the system, but Virginia herself faltered when the test came. No other Southern state ever seriously considered emancipation. Thus was the first step taken in the reduction of the slavery question to a sectional controversy.

In the next two decades the complete foundations of sectionalism were laid and the forces unloosed which drove the nation relentlessly forward toward a day of final reckoning. It was then that the fertile soil of the great Southwest and the insatiable demands of the European cotton mills truly made cotton king, fastened the shackles of slavery more securely upon two million human beings, introduced the horrible cruelty of the interstate slave trade, and replaced the attitude of apology for the institution with an aggressive defense of it as a positive good to both races. The status of the slaveholding planter had long been the social ideal in the South. It became increasingly so. Agrarianism versus industrialism had long been the dominant issue in national affairs. It was now intensified, though increasingly overshadowed and somewhat confused by the issue of slavery. Leadership of the agrarian party and, therefore, of the nation passed from the Virginians to representatives of the Black Belt. The roots of that party's philosophy were soon embedded in a slave economy. The rich heritage of social tradition implied by the term Jeffersonian democracy was prostituted to the perpetuation of class domination. Men opposed to slavery found the philosophy of the South so uncongenial and its tendencies so discouraging that, singly and en masse, they migrated to the North.

The Reverend Samuel Doak moved from Virginia to Little Limestone, near Jonesboro, Tennessee, and opened a school, called Martin Academy, in 1783. He freed his slaves;

sent them to Brown County, Ohio; and, until his death in 1830, indoctrinated his students with antislavery principles. The one student of prominence who remained in the South was Sam Houston, who went to Texas, became governor, and tried unsuccessfully to prevent the state from seceding in 1861. Gideon Blackburn became president of Centre College at Danville, Kentucky, and pastor of churches at Louisville and Versailles. In 1835 he assisted in founding Illinois College at Jacksonville, Illinois, and Blackburn College at Carlinville. John Rankin preached at Carlisle, Kentucky, from 1817 to 1821 and then moved to Ripley, Ohio, where he served as pastor of the Presbyterian Church for forty-four years. David Nelson was pastor of the Presbyterian Church at Danville, Kentucky, for many years, went to Marion College, near Palmyra, Missouri, and then to Carlinville, Illinois. James Gallagher moved to Cincinnati and became pastor of the Third Presbyterian Church in that city. Samuel Kelsey moved to Danville in 1809, where he served as pastor of the Presbyterian Church and was instrumental in founding Centre College before going to Marion College in 1828. Rankin joined with James H. Dickey and James Gilliland of South Carolina, Samuel Crothers of Kentucky, and Dyer Burgess in making the Chillicothe presbytery strongly antislavery and a tower of strength to Theodore Weld and James G. Birney in the thirties. Blackburn and Nelson worked with Birney in Kentucky and then came together again to assist Elijah P. Lovejoy and others in founding the antislavery society of Illinois in 1837.

Other prominent Southerners migrated during the period and became active abolitionists. James Lemen, close personal friend of Thomas Jefferson, moved from Virginia to Illinois and founded the first antislavery church, near Collinsville, in 1809. Edward Coles took his slaves from Virginia to Illinois in order to emancipate them, was elected to the governorship, and succeeded in keeping Illinois from

adopting a proslavery constitution in 1823. Angelina and
Sarah Grimké removed from Charleston, South Carolina, to
Philadelphia, then to Boston and, after Angelina's marriage
to Theodore Weld, to Fort Lee, New Jersey. Their lives
are forever identified with the crusade for peace, women's
rights, and emancipation. The Reverend George Bourne,
tried for heresy by his church assembly in Virginia, went to
Germantown, Pennsylvania, in 1817, devoted his life to antislavery publications, and assisted in founding the American
Anti-Slavery Society in 1833. William T. Allan and James
A. Thome, two of the greatest antislavery lecturers, were born
slaveholders, the former in Alabama, the latter in Kentucky.
William Ladd, president of the American Peace Society, had
been a slaveholder in Florida. Finally, there was James G.
Birney, of whom we shall have much to say later.

The importance of this migration cannot be overemphasized. It was the second phase of the development of a sectional alignment on the slavery question. It deprived the
South of men and women whose combined intelligence, moral
courage, and Christian benevolence would have gone far toward modifying the harsher features of slavery, toward preventing so great a unanimity of opinion in that section in
support of slavery as a positive good, and toward keeping
alive the spirit of free discussion. It brought together the
opponents of slavery from the South and those from New
England in the region west of the Alleghenies and north of
the Ohio, where they formed little islands of abolitionism at
an early date. It removed those who were instinctively opposed to slavery from its atmosphere, permitting them to
speak with far more freedom of its sordid aspects, and gave
to the abolition movement many of its most capable and
influential leaders. Having been born and reared in the
South, many of them as slaveholders, and having made great
personal sacrifices by migrating to the free states, they spoke

with authority and were given a respectful hearing by the conservative and wealthy class of people in the North.

The third phase of a developing sectionalism and the first phase of organized antislavery effort were combined in the activities of the American Colonization Society. The leading members of society at this time subscribed to the theory of biological inequality and racial inferiority of the Negroes. Men of every class joined in a common expression of contempt for them. Most Southern states prohibited manumission unless provision was made for their removal. Northern states met the challenge with oppressive legislation to discourage settlement. No one has ever more adequately described the status of free Negroes in the South than did the late Ulrich B. Phillips when he spoke of them as "a third element in a system planned for two." They were excluded from the schools, segregated in the cities, denied the franchise, forced into the less desirable occupations, registered and circumscribed within narrow limits, denied freedom of assemblage, and disciplined by the judicial processes of slavery rather than freedom. Their status in the North was, in many localities, little better than in the South, race prejudice operating through force of public opinion supplying the deficiencies of less severe legal restrictions.

Not without cause did the great British abolitionist, Charles Stuart, say in 1842 (and his observation would have been even more applicable ten years earlier): "Truly your country . . . is making itself more and more a spectacle equally disgusting and ridiculous to all independent and manly intelligences—applauding liberty, yet keeping slaves! Calling the slave trade piracy if practiced in Africa, but ready to wade thro' blood to honor and sustain it in America! Boasting of freedom, yet trampling upon free and generous discussion! Pretending to be brave, yet skulking like cowards from the light of truth! Professing religion, yet grasping . . . tenaciously . . . its gross idolatry of a white and its atrocious abhorrence of a colored skin!   The spires of its churches, pointing heavenward thro' the land; and the interior arrangements of its churches, proclaiming, not only without shame but boastfully, the dominion of Satan within.   The Ministers of its churches raging for doctrine, and contending with the zealot's zeal for their tithings of *mint, anise* and *cummin,* but contemptuously trampling upon the weightier matters of law, judgment, mercy and faith!   What a loathsome and portentous spectacle!   What a jest to demons!   What a grief to Angels, if Angels can mourn."[2]   That verbal castigation would appear to have been the peremptory pronouncement of an ill-informed religious fanatic; yet no man was better qualified to make it, by observation and by participation in the events of the previous decade, and we shall see how real was the basis for his indictment.

The presence of a Negro minority, first as slaves, then as free men, has always provided the acid test of American democracy.   That was particularly true when most Negroes were slaves, when the free among them were too scattered to develop their own economy, and when nearly all resided within the intellectually moribund and tradition-bound agricultural regions.   It was inevitable that men should have considered the possibility of their removal before entering upon the more difficult task of orientation which their continued presence would entail.   The American Society for the Colonization of the Free People of Color in the United States, commonly referred to as the American Colonization Society, was organized at Washington during the winter of 1816–17. The constitution of the society, unique in its brevity, was notable for three things: the exclusive function of the so-

---

[2] Charles Stuart to Theodore and Angelina Weld, February 21, 1842, in Barnes, Gilbert H., and Dumond, Dwight L., eds., *Letters of Theodore Dwight Weld, Angelina Grimké Weld, and Sarah Grimké, 1822–1844* (2 vols., New York, 1934), II, 928–929.   Hereafter cited as *Weld–Grimké Letters.*

ciety was the expatriation of free persons of color "with their consent"; there was an implied purpose to seek financial aid from the general and state governments; and there was no explanation of the motives for the concerted effort to remove Negroes from the country.

Were the importance of the society's activities from the date of organization until the outbreak of the Civil War to be judged solely by the acquisition of Liberia and the number of American Negroes sent there, it would merit no more than the passing notice that historians have customarily given it. In 1830 there were two million slaves in the United States, and the number was increasing by five hundred thousand every ten years. There were three hundred and nineteen thousand free persons of color, and their number was increasing by fifty thousand every ten years. Yet during the first twenty years of its activity the Colonization Society sent to Liberia fewer than four thousand emigrants. In 1832, the peak year and the date of greatest significance to our present study, the parent society and its two hundred and twenty-eight auxiliaries, with receipts of $43,000, succeeded in sending out only seven hundred and ninety-six emigrants, of which number Virginia alone supplied two hundred and thirty. Ohio, with seven auxiliaries in 1827 and thirty-seven in 1832, sent no emigrants before 1833, only forty-one in that year, and a total of fourteen more before 1860. Kentucky, with thirty-two auxiliaries by 1832, sent no emigrants before 1833, only ninety-nine that year, thirty-two in the next ten years, and fewer than six hundred by 1860. The number of emigrants was never large enough to satisfy the least sanguine expectation either of removing the free Negroes from the country or of eradicating slavery; but he who would discover the subtle forces which alter civilizations must view such organizations as this in their broader aspects and judge their significance by tests other than the fulfillment of avowed purposes.

In its inception the movement was inspired by a curious combination of humanitarianism, greed, and race prejudice. This was the era of benevolent enterprises, of which home and foreign missions, moral reform, temperance, and abolition of slavery were not the least.   Consider the constant appeal for funds and missionaries to Christianize the heathen, the belief that Negroes in the United States were destined to a permanent status of misery and degradation, the common knowledge of their propensity for vices which destroy the souls of men, the notion that the native habitat of the race would afford a more congenial environment for the development of latent talents, the repeated assertions that provision for the removal of emancipated slaves would accelerate manumission, faith in the ability of a nucleus of Christian Negroes in Africa to redeem the continent, and ask, What further appeal was necessary to bring to the support of the organization prominent men of means and humanitarian instincts?   Many of the influential abolitionists whose interest in the Negro question predated 1830, including Lewis Tappan, Gerrit Smith, James G. Birney, Theodore Weld, and Elizur Wright, were colonizationists in the earlier period. Their failure to give continued adherence to the enterprise derived from the conviction that something other than Christian benevolence inspired its origin and evolved from its continuance.

Few, if any, other institutions were ever so dependent as slavery upon tranquillity.   That tranquillity was secured, while slavery lasted, partially by a paralysis of public morality, partially by tolerance on the part of the non-slaveholder, and partially by repression.   Fewer than one third of the Southern people had any direct connection with slavery, but they were the important part, and they came close to constituting a ruling caste.   Even a passive attitude toward slavery placed the aspiring youth under suspicion, and less than commendation was a certain bar to public service, social approbation, or professional attainment. Hope of someday owning slaves, the patronizing attitude of slaveholders, satisfaction arising from one's ability to look down on others, and that undefinable something known as race prejudice caused those who owned no slaves to tolerate the system and indirectly to lend it their support. Draconian statutes and tolerance of extralegal action provided ample guarantee that the recalcitrant slave, the harborer of fugitives, and the instigator of insurrection would be summarily suppressed. Grant that there was a vast difference between the theory and the practical application of the slave codes; grant, also, that the danger of general insurrection was, and was known to be, remote; and the fact remains that slaveholders were afraid of a rational discussion of the merits of slavery. Almost from the first abolitionists and abolition literature were barred from the South, and fear that the Republicans would seek to build up their party organization there and thus introduce into the South itself widespread discussion of the slavery issue was a contributing cause to secession in 1861.

The presence of free Negroes was particularly annoying. Laws against manumission were designed to maintain the *status quo*. Society would not permit the owner to turn slaves loose to shift for themselves after they had passed the age of productive labor. Their maintenance was a fixed charge against production in good years and bad, in their youth and in their old age, in sickness and in health. There were, however, other reasons for the laws against manumission. The mere act of emancipation was looked upon as an implied censure of slavery, in the same sense as was the death penalty prescribed by federal law for engaging in the foreign slave trade. The mere presence of a free Negro community in a slave region was a source of disquietude and unrest among the slaves and a likely nursery for insurrection. There is no question that some humanitarian slaveholders wished to emancipate their slaves and to encourage others to do so, and that they supported the colonization movement for that reason; but, certainly, the generality of slaveholders anticipated greater security for the institution by the removal of a potentially dangerous element in the population.

In the North colonization had its support mainly among the aristocracy. It is extremely doubtful if race prejudice was based on social and economic rivalry between competing groups of whites and Negroes. The persecutions of free Negroes and abolitionists were not sudden outbursts of popular fury. Men of every social class, religion, and station in life were involved; and where the social aristocracy was not directly implicated, it contributed mightily by publicly winking at any action the ruffians might take. Greater than all other causes combined for the prevailing race prejudice among the intellectual and cultured classes of society was an uncritical acceptance of the theory of biological inequality and racial inferiority of the Negro. Ohio particularly and Pennsylvania and Connecticut to a lesser degree were strongholds of colonization societies whose object was not the emancipation of the slave or the elevation of the free blacks, but ridding the states of an undesirable and degraded element. Colonizationists hated abolitionists because abolitionists opposed colonization. They encouraged outrages against Negroes in order to discourage others from coming into the state. Theodore Weld, who braved the fury of countless mobs during those early years and knew, in an intimate way, the currents and crosscurrents of frontier society, was in Washington during the Cincinnati riots against the banks in 1842. Writing to his wife, Angelina Grimké Weld, he said: "A Cincinnati paper has just come to hand informing that a mob has been raging there for 6 hours. . . . They that sow the wind shall reap the whirlwind. The city authorities themselves, the bankers and brokers, were the leaders of the mob against the abolitionists. Now the cup of trembling is pressed to their own lips.    They raised the storm whose fury now spends itself on them."[3]

Three questions, then, present themselves for consideration:  (1) If the desire to be rid of the free Negroes was so prevalent in both sections of the country, why were so few emigrants sent out?    (2) Knowing the complete failure of the movement in that respect, why did people continue to give it support?    And (3) What is its historical importance?

The number of emigrants sent out was determined by the amount of available funds and by the willingness of Negroes to emigrate.   Nothing short of annual appropriations by Congress and the state legislatures could have provided an amount sufficient to colonize the annual increase of free Negroes at a cost of $80 per person.   Virginia and Maryland appropriated some money for the purpose; but, from the first, appeals to Congress were futile.   Here, as in every aspect of the slavery controversy, even the most remote from the direct question of emancipation, the extreme sensitiveness of the South was encountered.   Slavery was defended as a peculiar domestic institution, subject to regulation and control by no authority other than that of a state; and Southerners feared that appropriations by Congress for colonization would shortly lead to a discussion of slavery itself and to interference in the internal affairs of their section by the nation at large.   Reluctance to have the matter discussed and the fact that slaveholders, who controlled the state legislatures, bore the heavier burden of local taxation, forestalled all but infrequent, small contributions from the states.   The society was forced, therefore, to depend upon private contributions, which were scarcely more than sufficient to pay the cost of maintaining the organization.

Free Negroes were not disposed to go.   Of the 11,909

[3] Theodore D. Weld to Angelina G. Weld, January 15, 1842, *ibid.*, p. 894.

emigrants sent out by the parent society between 1820 and 1866, not more than 4,500 were born free, whereas 6,000 were emancipated for the purpose. Negroes, slaves as well as freemen, no less than whites, considered the United States their native land. It is difficult to conceive a more heart-rending experience than leaving in perpetuity one's native soil, relatives, friends, and occupation, whether it is done voluntarily or by compulsion. Forcing them to emigrate would have been greater cruelty than enslaving their ancestors in the beginning, and no state did so, though compulsory colonization was endorsed by many people and seriously debated in the legislatures of Virginia and Maryland. Intellectuals among the Negroes and abolitionists opposed colonization because it would drain away the most promising among them, to whom they looked for leadership in their program of emancipation and elevation of the race at home.

In fact, so little of a definite nature did colonization offer to the individual that nothing but proscription could have prompted even the few to venture upon the undertaking. "Free consent," as the term was used in the constitution of the Colonization Society, was little more than a jest. Abolitionists probably overemphasized the point in their attacks upon the society; but the man who had to choose between remaining in slavery or going to Africa as the price of emancipation can hardly be said to have been completely free in his choice. Nor does the term bear its usual connotation in the case of a free Negro living in constant fear of mob violence, denied the franchise, excluded from the schools, unrecognized in the courts of law, and deprived of the ordinary civilities and courtesies of his fellow men.

It is not difficult to understand why men continued to raise their voices in support of colonization in spite of its failure, even though less inclined to open their purses. It was not easy to choose between the two extremes in the slavery controversy. A man might not subscribe to the positive-good argument of the slaveholders and still be unwilling to endorse a program of unconditional immediate emancipation. Colonization presented the easy way out for that individual. It was a rationalization for the lazy intellect, a sedative for the guilty conscience, a refuge for the politician and the professional man. Therein lies much of the organization's historical importance. Abolitionists claimed that the only way to abolish slavery was to do it before proceeding to the task of elevating the race; that any consideration of particular plans for emancipation allowed the discussion to be drawn away from the main question and all sorts of extraneous issues to be introduced; that all talk of a preparatory process for freedom was absurd because the atmosphere of slavery was uncongenial to the development of individual traits essential to freedom; that only as a free man enjoying a full measure of civil rights could the Negro cultivate his mind, accumulate property, discipline his habits, and assume responsibilities so essential to correct social attitudes. The colonizationists could admit all these things, but hold that elevation of the Negro as a free man in the United States was as utterly impracticable as his elevation in slavery, and, thereby, indirectly support and perpetuate an institution admittedly wrong on moral grounds and inconsistent with the fundamental principles of American democracy.

Every appeal for funds and every exposition of the Society's objectives harped upon the depravity of the free Negroes, their hopeless situation, their ignorance, their misery, their lack of ability and ambition. Over and over again we find them designated in the official organ of the Society as "a mildew upon our fields," "a scourge to our backs," "a stain upon our escutcheon," "destitute of means, motives, and energy of character," "the most worthless and degraded portion of society," "greater nuisances than slaves," "most vicious, miserable people," "a vile excrescence upon society," "a curse and a contagion," "the most corrupt, depraved and abandoned race on earth," "a species of population pregnant with future danger and present inconvenience," "the outcasts of all society," and "more noxious than the slaves."

Nor did the colonizationists anticipate a change in the free Negroes' situation. The Connecticut society, in June, 1828, frankly stated: "Here the black man is degraded. You may call him free, you may protect his rights by legislation, you may invoke the spirit of humanity and of Christian benevolence to bless him, but still he is degraded. A thousand malignant influences around him are conspiring to wither all that is manly and noble in his nature."[4]  The editor of the *Snow Hill Messenger* of Maryland wrote, in deepest despondency: "This enormous empire of blacks rising up and putting on daily strength, having the shadow of liberty without the substance, is enough to make our children's children turn pale."[5]  As early as 1829 the American Colonization Society predicted that, "if the system, so long contended for by the uncompromising abolitionists could prevail, its effect would be to spread discord and devastation from one end of the Union to the other."[6]

The real historical significance of the colonization movement lies in this attitude toward free Negroes and abolitionists. The great obstacle to the emancipation and elevation of the Negro was the prevailing belief in racial inferiority and biological inequality. The constant repetition of that thesis, reworded and reëchoed in a thousand different ways, only served to strengthen race prejudice, increase contempt for the Negro on the part of the individual, and make more oppressive the existing Draconian statutes. It is not necessary to show that colonizationists openly abused abolitionists in order to prove that they were a retarding influence upon the antislavery movement. They never spoke favorably of abolitionists and, if they mentioned them at all, it was with con-

[4] *The African Repository and Colonial Journal* (Washington, 1825–89), IV, 118.          [5] *Ibid.*, p. 141.          [6] *Ibid.*, p. 363.

tempt.  The effect upon the little group of antislavery apostles was devastating.  Said Edward Beecher: "There is more
condensed venom in a few words of refined and pointed scorn,
uttered by some intelligent statesman or divine, than in whole
volumes of vulgar abuse.  Nothing is so malignant in its influence, nothing so hard to elude or to resist.  Now, when all
this withering influence is directed against a class of men
. . . against whom the odium of a work of reform which
touched the very vitals of the nation was rolling deep and
strong; what earthly power can withstand the shock?"[7]

At no time did those who adhered to the principle of
colonization lend their influence to the alleviation of the
Negroes' distress.  They did nothing to secure the repeal of
oppressive legislation in the free states; nothing to secure repeal of the laws against manumission; nothing to eliminate
abuses from the system of slavery and make it a humane and
civilizing institution; nothing to improve the economic status
of free Negroes in the North; nothing to provide for their
education or religious instruction; nothing to protect them
against kidnaping; nothing to defend their civil rights; nothing to prevent, if indeed they did not often incite, mob violence against both Negroes and abolitionists.  Considered in
all its aspects, the American Colonization Society was the
cohesive force for all the reactionary elements in the slavery
controversy.  Its steady decline began with its indictment by
the Lane Seminary students in Cincinnati in the winter of
1832–33.

That year marked the close of the preparatory period for
organized antislavery agitation on sectional lines.  Slavery
had been abolished in the Northern states; it was firmly entrenched in the Southern states, militantly defended by the
new leadership of the Black Belt, and presented not only as
a positive good to both races, but as a permanent solution of

[7] Beecher, Edward, *Narrative of Riots at Alton, in Connection with
the Death of Reverend Elijah P. Lovejoy* (Alton, 1838), p. 150.

the problem of racial adjustment.   Many outstanding opponents of slavery had removed from the South and were now withdrawing from the colonization movement, fully aware of the South's intention to perpetuate slavery and of the inadequacy of colonization as an antislavery enterprise. New organizations, with a new philosophy and with new objectives, were in the making.   Militant abolitionism was supplanting moderate antislavery doctrine in the Northern states, with the important new objective of elevating the Negroes in the United States instead of colonizing them in Africa.

## II. THE CINCINNATI–DANVILLE AXIS
### 1832–36

ON SEPTEMBER 15, 1834, James G. Birney and Theodore D. Weld met at a farmhouse twenty miles north of Georgetown, Kentucky. They had come on horseback, one from Danville, the other from Cincinnati, exercising care to prevent recognition and to preserve the utmost secrecy in their deliberations. Two years before Weld had been entertained at Birney's home in Huntsville, Alabama. Now, he feared to be seen with Birney in Kentucky lest his presence should add to the already heavy burden of opposition Birney was seeking to overcome. This was a day of confirmation. Both men had passed from hope to skepticism and then to outright disbelief in the efficacy of colonization. They had published their convictions; had pledged anew their faith in abolition; and had met again to plan the course of future action. Neither man yet knew the full measure of sacrifice it would entail, nor is it likely either cared.

Birney had always lived in solid comfort, if not in luxury. His father was a wealthy trader and rope manufacturer of Louisville. His relatives, his friends, and his professional associates all were members of the Southern aristocracy. He himself had been a slaveholding planter and prominent attorney in Huntsville. He had served in Alabama's first constitutional convention and had been intimately connected with the founding of its university. Had he remained in Alabama and loyal to his class, he would undoubtedly have risen to high position in public service. He was a man of indomitable courage and unyielding conviction, a devoted husband and father, an old-school Presbyterian, and a Whig of the landed-gentry vintage. Irish by birth, a humanitarian by instinct, a lawyer by training, he recognized no institutional authority of church, political party, or social caste to modify or to restrain one's individual responsibility to the celestial fire of conscience.

Weld was born in Connecticut and reared in western New York, the son of a conservative, small-town pastor. His formal education was meager, his learning prodigious, his powers of reasoning superb. While yet a young man he went about the western country lecturing upon manual laborism, the science of mnemonics, temperance and moral reform—an itinerant Socrates, with unkempt hair and beard and the simplest attire, caring only for personal cleanliness and the souls of men. He wrote of himself as "an untamed spirit, wild as the winds," stern, contemptuous of opposition, and "proud as Lucifer," "too proud to be *ambitious,* too proud to seek applause, too proud to tolerate it when lavished on me . . . too proud to *betray* emotions, too proud ever for an instant to loose my self possession whatever the peril, too proud ever to move a hair for personal interest, too proud ever to defend my character when assailed or my motives when impeached, too proud ever to *wince* even when the hot iron enters my soul and passes through it."[1] Gifted with rare powers of analysis and persuasion, a natural leader of men, he radiated his influence into every sphere of social reform. He was, in fact, the nerve center of the antislavery movement until the schism of 1840.

We do not know the precise date at which either man began to look askance at slavery, but it was early enough for them to have discussed the subject at length when Weld visited Huntsville in the spring of 1832. Birney's interest arose from personal knowledge of the sordid aspects of the institution, concern for the future of his young sons, an intense patriotism that saw in slavery a cancerous growth within

[1] Theodore D. Weld to Angelina Grimké, March 1, 1838, *Weld–Grimké Letters,* II, 576–577.

the body politic, and the common fear that Negro concentration would overwhelm the lower South. It was sufficiently well known for the Colonization Society to offer him the general agency for the southwestern states on June 12, 1832. Weld was the protégé of Charles Stuart, who financed his education, interested him in the slavery question, and was the one living man to whom he bared his heart and made obeisance; but their early association was as members of Charles Grandison Finney's band of revivalists, and Weld's fame as an orator was established before Stuart himself turned to the question of slavery. Weld's trip in 1832 was in behalf of Oneida Institute and manual laborism particularly, and of a prospective theological seminary incidentally. As early as March, 1830, Stuart had been writing to interest Weld in slavery; Weld joined with Tappan, Jocelyn, Goodell, and others in a discussion of the subject in 1831; and he turned aside on his journey in 1831–32 to indoctrinate the faculty at Western Reserve College, including Beriah Green, Elizur Wright, and President George Storrs; but in what? In opposition to slavery, of course, though certainly not in hostility to colonization and an endorsement of immediate emancipation of slaves to be retained and elevated among their former masters, because he wrote to Birney in September, 1832, from Cincinnati: "When I look at the great slave question, trace its innumerable and illimitable bearings upon the weal of the world, every year augmenting its difficulties, its dangers, its woe and its guilt, my heart aches with hope deffered [sic], mocks all prescriptions and refuses to be comforted. I am ripe in the conviction that if the Colonization Society does not dissipate the horror of darkness which overhangs the southern country, we are undone. Light breaks *in from no other quarter.*"[2]

[2] Theodore D. Weld to James G. Birney, September 27, 1832, in Dumond, Dwight L., ed., *Letters of James Gillespie Birney, 1831–1857* (2 vols., New York, 1938), I, 27. Hereafter cited as *Birney Letters.*

Birney, in the interim, had abandoned his legal practice and for one year strove mightily to convert the Southwest to the cause of colonization. Like Weld, he was opposed to slavery, but an immediate emancipationist could hardly have written: "If the abolitionist be really desirous of bene-fitting his fellowmen, and of advancing the cause of human happiness . . . we would invite him to visit those parts of the *South,* where there is, already, a large proportion of the free colored class. If he be diligent, judicious and dispassionate, we risk nothing in saying, that he will be convinced of the superior wisdom of trying every other plan, bearing upon its face the least appearance of feasibility, before experiment be made of his favorite *Abolition*."[3]

The point I wish to make is that, to say a man was op-posed to slavery means very little except that he was not a devotee of the positive-good argument. There was a vast difference between antislavery and abolition. The tests of abolitionism were: (1) willingness by those who owned no slaves to bring about a state of emancipation by compulsion; (2) refusal to countenance expatriation; and (3) insistence upon according to the emancipated slaves all the privileges and civil liberties of free men. Neither Weld nor Birney was an abolitionist in the summer of 1832, though they were to play the stellar rôles in the great human drama of the next decade.

The two years between these conferences—July, 1832, and September, 1834—was a preparatory period for the complete acceptance of abolition doctrine, a period in which they were convinced: (1) that colonization was impracticable; that its moving impulse was race prejudice; that it was strengthening rather than weakening the institution of slavery; that it was economically unsound and morally wrong; (2) that slave-holders would never voluntarily enter upon a program even

---

[3] James G. Birney, "Colonization of the Free Colored People, No. 6," in the *Democrat* (Huntsville, Ala.), June 20, 1833.

of gradual emancipation; and (3) that the display of intoler-
ance which greeted the mildest discussion of the subject lifted
the controversy from the realm of specific reform in a particular section and presaged another episode in the ageless
struggle for human rights. Would that the historian might
somehow recover the emotions which surge through men's
hearts and alter civilizations! It was only a short decade
from the day that Birney turned his attention to colonization
until he was nominated for the presidency by the Liberty
Party, but it was a decade replete with as choice a repertoire
of human drama as the nation has ever produced.

Birney's work as agent for the Colonization Society need
not detain us long. Its tangible results were negligible: the
organization of a few scattered auxiliary societies, the launching of a small parcel of emigrants on the steamer *Ajax* from
New Orleans, the publication of a series of fifteen essays on
the subject, the delivery of many lectures to mere handfuls
of listeners. He discovered a total lack of interest in the
subject on the part of both Negroes and whites. Few came
to hear him lecture. Newspapers were reluctant to publish
his expositions, and only the first seven were reprinted in
the official organ of the parent society. Friends implored
him to abandon a hopeless cause. Finally, he admitted failure, resigned his agency, severed old friendships, and in September, 1833, sought the hoped-for congenial atmosphere
of Danville, Kentucky, scene of his childhood days. On
December 11, 1833, he expressed the opinion in a letter to
R. R. Gurley, general secretary of the American Colonization
Society, that slavery was "altogether un-Christian"; that it
would ruin the country unless speedily abolished; and that
it was futile to expect its elimination through colonization.
Gurley replied to Birney with an amazingly prophetic letter,
saying in part: "I deeply regret that there should exist so
much apathy, indeed may I not say error of opinion, on the
subject of slavery at the South. . . . My own opinion is, that

the South must, if its own dearest interests are to be preserved, if the Union is to last, act with vastly more zeal and energy on this subject than has yet been manifested. . . . I hope all this may be done. But I have many fears it will not be effectually done. . . . If it be once understood that the South designs to *perpetuate* Slavery, the whole North will be speedily organized into Anti-Slavery Societies, and the whole land will be flooded with anti-slavery publications."[4]

Almost at the time these letters were written—early December, 1833—a number of gentlemen near Danville formed the Kentucky Society for the Gradual Relief of the State from Slavery, pledging themselves to emancipate all slaves born thereafter when they reached the age of twenty-five years. The Address of the Society signed by John Green, but almost certainly written by Birney, contains some surprisingly advanced doctrine. Of slavery it said: "The sentence of condemnation has been passed upon it by the *Civilized World;* and we venture the opinion that no respectable person will be found in our State, to arraign the decision." The introduction of slavery and its continuance were denounced as "violations of the law of nature," but the latter was the greater wrong because of our "enjoying the full blaze of that light which our own revolution and other similar events have thrown upon the principles of civil and religious liberty—by us who hold up our institutions as patterns from which the statesmen and patriots of other nations are invited to copy, and who boast our country to be the freest on the Globe, and an asylum for the oppressed of every other."

The fundamental principle of the association was stated to be: "That domestic slavery, as it exists under the laws and constitution of this state—perpetual and absolute,—is a great moral and political evil; and that its continuance cannot be justified, before God, the world, or our own consciences, any

[4] Ralph R. Gurley to James G. Birney, December 17, 1833, *Birney Letters,* I, 110.

longer than is necessary to bring it to a termination, less injurious to the parties, than slavery itself."

Repudiating general emancipation without previous preparation as a "wild experiment—endangering the peace and security of the whites, and the very existence of the colored race," it presented the Society's program as *"immediate* preparation for *future* emancipation," justifying it on the ground "that *adequate preparation* for that kind of future gradual emancipation, which will operate beneficially to both the master and slave, can be successfully *commenced* in no other way, than by deciding *first, that slavery shall cease to exist—absolutely, unconditionally, and irrevocably.* When that is settled, then, and not till then, *the whole community* [of whites] *will feel a common interest, in making the best possible preparation for the event."*[5]

On December 4 there was organized at Philadelphia the American Anti-Slavery Society, whose doctrine was immediate emancipation, defined as gradual emancipation immediately begun. Professor Gilbert H. Barnes has interpreted this straitened use of the term as an effort to bring British precedent to the movement's support and as realization by its sponsors of the difficulty of applying imperial methods in a country whose general government was one of distinctly limited and delegated powers. Without denying the validity of that interpretation, may I venture to assert that the eastern men were probably no further advanced in their opinions than the Kentuckians, though less gifted with clarity of expression. I have never seen a more crystal-clear statement of what the antislavery leaders of the next ten years were trying to accomplish than the Kentucky statement of the indispensable prerequisite of any program: the decision *"first, that slavery shall cease to exist—absolutely, unconditionally, and irrevocably."*

[5] "Constitution and Address of the Kentucky Society for the Gradual Relief of the State from Slavery," *ibid.,* pp. 99–109.

Before leaving Alabama Birney had abandoned hope for the redemption of the lower South and all his life felt that that region eventually would be overwhelmed by Negroes and abandoned by the whites.  He urged Gurley to concentrate all efforts on Kentucky, Virginia, and Maryland, holding that the slave power would collapse and the Union be saved if these states could be induced to get rid of their slaves.  He labored indefatigably during the winter of 1833–34 to win his own state to a program of gradual emancipation, lecturing at Frankfort, Louisville, and Lexington with Judge John Green and President John Young of Centre College.  Many others, including Professor James Buchanan, President Luke Munsell of the Danville Deaf and Dumb Asylum, the Reverend David Nelson of the Danville Presbyterian Church, and Dr. David Bell, lent their moral support and personal influence.  The effort was unavailing, though little organized opposition was encountered, and Birney took the final step of repudiating both colonization and gradualism.  Meanwhile events of far-reaching import had occurred at Cincinnati.  The students of Lane Seminary, gathered from all parts of the country, were making history under the guiding genius of Weld.

Cincinnati contained more than one-third of the seventy-five hundred Negroes in the state of Ohio, many of whom were emancipated slaves who had been or were then paying for themselves or for their friends or relatives still in bondage.  No other place in the United States offered a better opportunity to test the ability of the Negro to make advancement if given the opportunity.  Into this mass of humanity these students had thrown themselves without restraint and had established Sabbath schools, day and evening schools, a lyceum where they lectured four evenings a week on grammar, geography, arithmetic, natural philosophy, etc.  They mingled freely with the Negro population, relieving distress and cultivating intellectual and moral progress, and incidentally furnishing an excuse for the revival of mob violence.

They organized a college lyceum and discussed at length the question of slavery in all its aspects, with particular emphasis upon colonization and emancipation. Colonization was repudiated as unworthy of the support and patronage of Christians, and immediate emancipation was endorsed. There then ensued the first and one of the greatest contests for academic freedom in the history of the country.

The students had given a practical demonstration in refutation of the prevailing belief that Negroes were inherently incapable of advancement and destined by nature to a position of inferiority. They had pooled their intimate knowledge of slavery gained by long residence in the slave states, had reasoned and rationalized as became gentlemen trained in the school of the Great Revival, and had concluded that slavery was a sin great enough to justify their undivided attention.

Thirty members of this theological class were over twenty-six years of age, fourteen were over twenty-eight, and nine were between thirty and thirty-five. All were college graduates, most of them having received degrees from eight to seventeen years previously. Six were married men. One was a practicing physician, and twelve had been public lecturers of prominence. They had come to Lane Seminary perfectly cognizant of the strategic location of the institution. J. L. Tracy, a former schoolmate of Weld at Oneida Institute, then teaching at Lexington, Kentucky, had written to Weld, November 24, 1831: "You are well aware of the fact that this western country is soon to be a mighty giant that shall wield not only the destinies of our own country but of the world. 'Tis yet a babe. Why not then come and take it in the feebleness of its infancy and give a right direction to its powers, that when it grows up to its full stature we may bless God that it has such an influence?"[6] The students themselves declared: "The Valley was our expected

[6] J. L. Tracy to Theodore D. Weld, November 24, 1831, *Weld–Grimké Letters*, I, 57.

field; and we assembled here, that we might the more accurately learn its character, catch the spirit of its gigantic enterprise, grow up in its genius, appreciate its peculiar wants, and be thus qualified by practical skill, no less than by theological erudition, to wield the weapons of truth."[7]

Here in Cincinnati, the most strategic location in the United States, was a new theological seminary with as fine a body of young men as any school in the country, as proved by testimony of their president and by their later accomplishments, and with the possibility of becoming the center of the intellectual and cultural life of the entire valley. Yet all but two or three of the faculty and trustees were so blinded by race prejudice, so devoted to the cause of colonization, so sensitive to popular clamor, and so destitute of knowledge about the true purpose of the educational process as to proscribe the right of free discussion. The students were commanded to discontinue their antislavery society and prohibited from holding meetings and from discussing the subject even at the dinner table. A committee was vested with discretionary power of dismissal. Almost the entire student body requested honorable dismissal. The faculty granted it, but thereafter threw every possible obstacle in the way of the work they were seeking to accomplish. Filled with the glorious vigor of youth, the fervor of religious conviction, and the enthusiasm of the crusader in a worthy cause, the rebels redoubled their efforts among the Negro population, pursued their studies independently, and, finally, went to Oberlin College, where Asa Mahan served as president and Finney came to head theology. But, leaving, they hurled defiance at the faculty in words that stand out as one of the greatest prophecies of the century:

"Sirs, you have mistaken alike the cause, the age and the

---

[7] [Weld, Theodore D.], *A Statement of the Reasons Which Induced the Students of Lane Seminary to Dissolve Their Connection with That Institution* (Cincinnati, 1834), p. 3.

men, if you think to intimidate by threats, or to silence by clamor, or shame by sneers, or put down by authority, or discourage by opposition, or appal by danger, those who have put their hands to this work. . . . Slavery, with its robbery of body and soul from birth to death, its exactions of toil unrecompensed, its sunderings of kindred, its frantic orgies of lust, its intellect levelled with dust, its baptisms of blood, and its legacy of damning horrors to the eternity of the spirit —Slavery, in this land of liberty and light . . . its days are numbered and well-nigh finished. . . . The nation is shaking off its slumbers to sleep no more."[8]

Meanwhile, Birney, within four months of the date of launching the Kentucky Society for the Gradual Relief of the State from Slavery, became convinced, as he says, that slavery was sinful, although only a hairsplitting divine could explain how a man who had spoken of slavery as unchristian, morally wrong, and a greater evil than original enslavement needed to be convinced that slavery was a sin. What is probably more nearly the truth was Birney's conviction that only through an appeal to the conscience of the slaveholder by preaching the sin of slavery could anything be gained. Early in May, 1834, before the students dispersed for vacation, and previous to the faculty action proscribing academic freedom, Birney wrote his famous "Letter on Colonization, Addressed to the Rev. Thornton J. Mills, Corresponding Secretary of the Kentucky Colonization Society," and followed it shortly with his "Letter to the Ministers and Elders on the Sin of Holding Slaves, and the Duty of Immediate Emancipation." The first was published in the Lexington *Intelligencer,* the second in the Cincinnati *Journal,* and thousands of copies were mailed by the students to ministers and prominent laymen in the Mississippi Valley. They were promptly reprinted in the New York *Evangelist*

[8] Theodore D. Weld to James Hall, May 20, 1834, *Weld–Grimké Letters,* I, 146.

and the *Emancipator,* and as separate pamphlets by the American Anti-Slavery Society.

Birney and Weld were in constant communication during the summer months (1834). Birney decided to abandon everything else and to devote his life to antislavery work. Arrangements were made for his support by the national society, and it was agreed that he remain in Kentucky, organize a state antislavery society, and establish an antislavery newspaper. He was to labor with the Presbyterian synod of the state to secure antislavery resolutions. Weld was to circle through Ohio and Pennsylvania to Pittsburgh and attend the general assembly there, make arrangements for the organization of an Ohio antislavery society, secure subscriptions to Birney's paper, and return by way of Marietta and Steubenville. The conference near Georgetown in September put the finishing touches to these plans.

During the winter months the Lane rebels trekked to Oberlin, and Weld blazed a trail of abolitionism across Ohio and Pennsylvania. Birney quietly went about his task in Kentucky, organizing the state antislavery society at Danville on March 18, 1835, with James Buchanan as president and Luke Munsell as secretary, publishing a prospectus of his proposed paper—the *Philanthropist*—and making arrangements for printing at the office of the *Olive Branch* in Danville. Then the storm broke.

Thirty-three gentlemen of standing addressed to Birney, on July 12, 1835, a sharp remonstrance against the publication of his paper. Deprecating the failure of the legislature to have laws against such incendiary publications passed—whether from the feeling that none so base could be found in Kentucky society or from the belief that the Negroes were too illiterate to cause concern, or from a desire to preserve the freedom of the press—they requested that Birney forbear until legislation could be secured which would prevent his publication and thus obviate the necessity of resort to mob violence. Birney's reply was a denial of legislative power to interfere with the constitutional guarantee of freedom of the press; a defense of the value of discussion concerning matters of great moment to the people; an assertion that discussion had already begun, would continue, and would be dangerous to the peace of society only if forced underground, concealed, and surreptitiously carried on; and a warning that silence in the slave states would increase discussion in the free states.

Both communications were published in the *Olive Branch,* and the slaveholders, firm in their position that "no *American Slaveholding Community* has found itself able to bear" the experiment of free discussion, called a public meeting at the Baptist Church on July 25. James Barbour, president of the Branch Bank of Kentucky and treasurer of Centre College, presided. The Reverend J. K. Burch, moderator of the Presbyterian synod of Kentucky, was a principal speaker. The meeting, probably of five hundred, left no doubt of its determination to resort to mob violence if necessary to prevent publication of the *Philanthropist,* and passed a series of resolutions denouncing it as a scheme "wild, visionary, impracticable, unpolitical, and contrary to the spirit of our laws, and at war with the spirit of our Constitution." Four days later a mob assembled to destroy the press, but dispersed when its former owner, a member of their own party, took possession of the establishment.

That day marked the end of the organized antislavery movement in Kentucky. Within a month Birney moved his family to Cincinnati. The Reverend David Nelson published a blistering farewell sermon to his congregation and moved to Marion College, Missouri, but was forced to seek safety for himself and family at Carlinville, Illinois. Professor Buchanan accepted a professorship at Oberlin, remained a term, and then also went to Carlinville. Here they joined with the Reverend Robert Holman, Birney's old

friend of Huntsville, Alabama, Elijah Lovejoy, and Edward
Beecher in founding the Illinois Anti-Slavery Society. Luke
Munsell moved to Indianapolis, assisted in organizing the
Indiana State Anti-Slavery Society, and became its first president. Of the little coterie only President Young remained,
in his heart an abolitionist, openly supporting gradualism,
secretly keeping up his contact with Birney.

As for the Lane rebels, it would be difficult to overesti-
mate the influence of these two years. They served as agents
of the American Anti-Slavery Society in 1836, abolitionized
Ohio, and then formed the nucleus of the famous "Seventy."
Henry B. Stanton was financial and corresponding secretary
of the American Anti-Slavery Society, an active member of
the Free Soil Party, and editor of the New York *Sun*. Asa
Mahan became successively president of Oberlin College,
Cleveland University, and Adrian College. James A. Thome
taught for many years at Oberlin, wrote, with Horace Kim-
ball, the powerful tract *Emancipation in the West Indies,* and
served influential pastorates in Cleveland and at Mount
Vernon. Philemon Bliss entered Congress from Elyria,
Ohio, became chief justice of Dakota Territory and dean of
the Law School of the University of Missouri. George
Whipple became professor of mathematics at Oberlin, secretary of the American Missionary Association, and a partic-
ipant in the Freedman's Aid. Augustus Wattles spent a
fortune and the best years of his life teaching free Negroes
to become economically self-sufficient, and edited the *Herald
of Freedom* in Kansas during that territory's troublous years.
Marius Robinson founded and edited until 1861 the *Anti-
Slavery Bugle* at Salem, Ohio, and then became president of
the Ohio Mutual Fire Insurance Company. Hiram Wilson
directed for many years the work of rehabilitation of fugitive
slaves in Canada. Hiram Foote, Edward Weed, Calvin
Waterbury, John W. Alvord, William T. Allen, and others
held prominent pastorates in the West after the agency phase

of the movement had been supplanted by political agitation. Professor Calvin Stowe, who "came right" on the question within a few months after the Lane debate, married Harriet Beecher, moved to far-off Andover, and from the recollections of these stirring days came *Uncle Tom's Cabin*.

Judged only by the training of these early apostles of freedom, the events of the two years at Danville and Cincinnati would merit the attention of historians. More important still, they gave character and direction to the movement, making it a powerful religious crusade in the direction of moral reform. It was theological students in a theological seminary, drawing their inspiration largely from the great revival, who sat in judgment on the institution of slavery. Weld and Stanton selected the "Seventy" and rarely departed from type in the selection of agents. From first to last churches were the forums, preachers the most consistent and powerful advocates, and the sin of slavery the cardinal thesis of the new social philosophy. The religious character of the antislavery meetings, the Christian piety, meekness, and humility of the pioneer abolition lecturers, the religious fanaticism which soon enshrouded the entire movement, the particular instructions of the central committee to agents in the field to "insist principally on the *sin of slavery,* because our main hope is in the consciences of men, and it requires little logic to prove that it is always safe to do right," and the intimate notes from one to another, every line of which is a prayer in itself, leave no doubt as to the true character of the first phases of the movement. Birney's emphasis upon the incompatibility of slavery and the fundamental philosophy on which the nation was established blossomed eventually, through his leadership, as the principle upon which Northern sectionalism sought to administer the government.

Finally, the exile of Birney, the very soul of dignity, integrity, and Christian virtue, from his native state and the proscription of academic freedom at Lane Seminary established precedents and enthroned a principle: the slaveholders' interests were paramount and their fiat was law.  Birney's perspective was never clearer than when he wrote to Gerrit Smith: "It is as much as all the patriotism in our country can do, to keep alive the spirit of liberty in the *free states.* The contest is becoming—has become—one, not alone of freedom for the *black,* but of freedom for the *white.*  It has now become absolutely necessary, that slavery should cease in order that freedom may be preserved to any portion of our land.  The antagonist principles of liberty and slavery have been roused into action and one or the other must be victorious.  There will be no cessation of the strife until Slavery shall be exterminated or liberty destroyed."[9]

[9] James G. Birney to Gerrit Smith, September 13, 1835, *Birney Letters,* I, 343.

# III. THE ABOLITION INDICTMENT OF SLAVERY

NO OTHER reform movement is quite like the antislavery crusade, because it was based upon an appeal to the consciences of men; yet the sinners were almost wholly insulated from the preachment, and the anxious seat was crowded with saints, so that the historian is tempted to agree with Pascal, that "There are but two classes of men, the righteous, who think themselves to be sinners, and the sinners, who think themselves righteous." One *expects* to find the contemporary literature of the great controversy strongly biased, but race prejudice still lives, and the writings of trained historians, also, have such an overtone of moralizing or apology as to leave the impression their wishes determined what they should accept as truth. Fortunately, we do not need to agree on the precise nature of American Negro slavery. Historians have too long focused their attention upon that controversial point, to the neglect of more important things. One can no more describe the life of the slave than describe a typical plantation. There was too much diversity, and the human element entered in too largely to permit even a highly centralized picture. To attempt it is to become lost in a labyrinth of qualifications. Abolitionists omitted the qualifications and strengthened their case accordingly, but weakened it in the light of historical research.

One may find in abolition literature, not here and there but in dreary succession, charges of vilest depravity: miscegenation between owners, owners' sons, and overseers—whom Birney called the "feculum" of society—and the female slaves, with all the accompanying tragedies of mixed blood, sale of children by their fathers, pollution of men's souls and degradation of the home; slave breeding, ranging from the encouragement of promiscuity and inducements for continuous bearing of children, to compulsory submission to service by Negroes and whites of fine physique and degenerate character; separation of families, of husbands and wives, brothers and sisters, and children of tender age from mothers, either from financial stringency, liquidation of estates, or downright disregard of human feelings; virtual freedom to comely young females willing to prostitute themselves and share their earnings; mutilation of bodies, in anger, in search of punishment equal to the nature of the offense, or in satisfaction of sadistic impulses; branding, shackling, placing in stocks, burdening with iron collars, chains, etc., to prevent running away; criminal neglect of the injured, the seriously ill, and the incurably diseased for the sake of economy; and the merciless hunting down of fugitives with bloodhounds and guns, with the levity and zest of the possum hunt.

The weakness of this sort of propaganda lay in the necessity (1) for a constant increase in the enormity of the offense charged; (2) for variation, since attention was more easily arrested by the novelty of the guilt than by its degree; and (3) for unimpeachable supporting evidence to satisfy the skeptic. Some of the pornographic calendar is so stereotyped in form as to bear the impress of legend. Some of it was hearsay, undoubtedly magnified in the telling. The more repulsive incidents were of uncommon occurrence and were no more authentic criteria by which to judge the institution as a whole than was Jefferson Davis' experiment in self-government for his slaves. It was the sort of stuff that warms the heart of the true propagandist and fascinates the sanctimonious pietist as well as the irreligious miscreant. But such aspects of slavery as miscegenation, separation of families, cruel punishments, and barbarous treatment of fugitives cannot be minimized either by one who seeks a true picture of slavery or by one who seeks the causes of the Civil

War. Historians have no justification for ignoring abolition literature in their work on slavery. The great bulk of this part of it was written by high-minded men and women who were either born and reared in the South or had lived there many years. One would hardly expect to find mention of these sordid aspects of the institution in plantation records, in private diaries or letters, or in treatises written in defense of slavery. The fact that Southerners who did write about them were living at the time in states where there was no slavery does not detract from, but rather increases, the probability of their accuracy. Supported, as they were, by certain other indisputable facts we shall shortly refer to, they would have given all but the most obdurate champions of slavery cause for serious reflection; but the generality of Southerners had not the slightest conception of abolition arguments or of the principles for which they were contending.

The restlessness of slaveholders over colonization activities crystallized into a militant defense of slavery as antislavery agitation increased in the North—a defense which denied freedom of speech and of the press, excluded abolition literature from the mails, and drove everyone suspected of heresy out of the South, and hence closed the public forums to all antislavery doctrine. At the same time the fulminations of those abolitionists who allowed their opposition to slavery to lead them along the psychopathic trail to a hatred of slaveholders and who took special delight in foul invective and ribald abuse of everyone connected with the institution were copied into the Southern newspapers as a warning of the impending Northern plague. Perhaps it was inevitable that men who hated slavery should hate slaveholders. Perhaps it is just to lump the sinner with the sin. That is a matter of opinion. In any case it was not conducive to calm reflection or sympathetic understanding or a peaceable solution of the question. Year after year the

Southerners went on enduring these charges of moral turpitude, with their holier-than-thou implications, nursing their wrath, and finding consolation in self-justification.

This catalogue of specific wrongs was also a part of the more general indictment of slavery as a sin. The antislavery movement was a powerful religious crusade, and religion played a far more important part in American life then than it does today. The Bible was presented as irrefutable proof that Jesus taught a doctrine of universal brotherhood; that man was created in the image of God; and that slavery reduced him to a piece of merchandise to be bought and sold in the market place. Said Theodore Weld, when the American Anti-Slavery Society was organized: "God has committed to every moral agent the privilege, the right and the responsibility of personal ownership. This is God's plan. Slavery annihilates it, and surrenders to avarice, passion and lust, all that makes life a blessing. It crushes the body, tramples into the dust the upward tendencies of the intellect, breaks the heart and kills the soul."[1] Said the Central Executive Committee: "Every man who has put on the armor of Jesus Christ is under the paramount pledge to do all in his power for the salvation of the souls for which He died. How can you, my brother, do more than by *now* espousing the cause of those for whose souls there are *no men* to care."[2] Slavery was denounced as a sin, "always, everywhere and only sin," *aside* from the evils of its administration. Abolitionists demanded that slaveholders be excluded from the pulpits of Northern churches and from the privileges of the sacraments, and those Southerners who finally championed the cause of secession lingered long on this aspect of the cause for action. Said the distinguished John S. Preston of South Carolina be-

[1] Theodore D. Weld to Arthur Tappan, Joshua Leavitt, and Elizur Wright, Jr., November 22, 1833, *Weld–Grimké Letters*, I, 120.

[2] Elizur Wright, Jr., to Theodore D. Weld, December 31, 1833, *ibid.*, p. 122.

fore the Virginia Convention: "This diversity at this moment is appearing not in forms of denominational polemics, but in shapes as bloody and terrible as religion has ever assumed since Christ came to earth. Its representative, the Church, has bared her arm for the conflict—her sword is already flashing in the glare of the torch of fanaticism—and the history of the world tells us that when that sword cleaves asunder, no human surgery can heal the wound. There is not one Christian slaveholder here, no matter how near he may be to his meek and lowly master, who does not feel in his heart that from the point of that sword is now dripping the last drop of sympathy which bound him to his brethren at the North. With demoniac rage they have set the Lamb of God between their seed and our seed."[3]

In support of their charge that these violations of the standards of contemporary civilization were far more prevalent than Southerners were willing to admit, were inherent in slavery, and were indicative of the general moral tone of the institution, abolitionists presented a line of argument which was not easily contradicted. Slaves were property. They were bought and sold. The purchase price alone determined who might be a slaveholder. Society set no standards of intelligence, character, or integrity for slaveholding. There were no public or private agencies charged with responsibility for the slave's welfare. Human nature being what it is or, better still, what it then was, what security was there for the individual slave against abuse of arbitrary power? Said Weld: "Arbitrary power is to the mind what alcohol is to the body; it intoxicates. It is perhaps the strongest human passion; and the more absolute the power, the stronger the desire for it; and the more it is desired, the

[3] *Addresses Delivered by Hon. Fulton Anderson, Commissioner from Mississippi, Hon. Henry L. Benning, Commissioner from Georgia, and Hon. John S. Preston, Commissioner from South Carolina, before the Virginia State Convention, February 1, 1861* (Charleston, 1861), p. 61.

more its exercise is enjoyed. . . .   The fact that a person intensely desires power over others, *without restraint,* shows
the absolute necessity of restraint."[4] This condition was
greatly aggravated by the fact that slaves were subject not
only to the will of their owner, but to the authority of every
white person with whom they came in contact off the owner's
property, and to the slightest whim of the owner's family,
even of children too immature to have disciplined themselves; and by the further fact that, in spite of abject servility
and personal desire to suppress emotions, evidences of resent-
ment must have been a common occurrence. "The idea
of *property* having a will," said Weld, "and that too in opposition to the will of its *owner,* and counteracting it, is a
stimulant of terrible power to the most relentless human
passions."[5]   In support of his logic he brought together in
*American Slavery As It Is* what he chose to call the "testimony of a thousand witnesses," the most devastating arraign-
ment of slavery ever published.   Hundreds of thousands of
copies of the pamphlet were distributed, and its influence
was incalculable.   There was no effective reply to it, nor
could there have been.

Not only did abolitionists examine slavery in the light
of the Scriptures and of the moral standards prevailing in
contemporary civilization; they also pronounced it contrary
to the fundamental principles of the American way of life
because it plundered the slaves of their inalienable rights
as men: ownership of their own bodies; freedom of choice
as to use of time and to occupation; the rights of marriage,
family life, and paternal authority; the right to worship according to conscience; the right to cultivate their minds,
utilize their peculiar talents and influence their fellow men;
the right to protect themselves, their homes, and their families against violence; the right to the protection of the law.

[4] [Weld, Theodore D.], *American Slavery As It Is* (New York, 1839),
p. 115.                              [5] *Ibid.,* p. 111.

These were things which, especially in those days of rugged individualism, made a powerful impression upon the average American.

The lack of legal protection for the slave constituted the greatest single indictment against the slaveholding states. The slave owner had no restraint but his own will over the type and amount of labor assigned to tne slave. He might hire him out to other men; he might permit him to labor on his own account and claim his wages; he might inflict any kind or degree of punishment without fear of redress; he might assign absolute authority over the slave to any agent. He might sell the slave at will. The slave was both a chattel and real estate and liable to be sold in satisfaction of debts. He could not testify in court in any case involving a white man. If he raised his hand against a white man in any circumstances whatsoever, the penalty was death. He had no recourse against intolerable conditions but perilous flight. He could own no property, make no contracts, receive no education, claim no religious instruction. Whatever legislation had been passed with respect to slaves was purely for protection of property rights and the security of the institution. One may find, only rarely, feeble recognition by legislatures and courts of slaves as human beings. This was slavery's most vulnerable spot and was so considered by the abolitionists.

The practical application of the law, said the apologists for slavery, was far less rigorous than the provisions of the law, which was simply ignoring the point at issue. When they spoke of the slave codes as being unenforced except at rare intervals when mass hysteria followed attempted insurrections, a particularly brutal murder, or the apprehension of a suspected incendiary, they were speaking of laws passed for the protection of society, i.e. laws forbidding slaves to assemble without the presence of a white person; forbidding slaves to leave their owners' premises without a written permit; forbidding slaves to preach or masters to teach them to read; and requiring the regular patrol of all public highways.   The important point is that that great body of law, both common and statute, and the courts, the instrument of its operation, to which men have looked since time immemorial for the administration of justice and for the protection of their most elementary human rights simply did not exist for three million slaves.   Privileges they might have and no doubt did enjoy in generous measure from indulgent masters, but they had no more semblance of rights than the beasts of the field.

More difficult to evaluate with respect to its place in the Northern educational program was the abolition argument concerning the effect of slavery upon the two races and upon the South from the viewpoint of general culture and economy.   This was in the nature of a rebuttal to the positive-good argument, the development of which preceded the abolition crusade of the thirties.   The positive-good dogma embraced four theses: (1) that slave labor was essential to the development and continued prosperity of the southern country; (2) that the Negro race was inferior and destined by nature to a subordinate position; (3) that slavery had lifted a savage people from barbarism to Christian civilization; and (4) that the white race had not degenerated as a consequence, but, on the contrary, had developed a unique and high degree of culture.   Ancillary to these there were, of course, a number of supporting theses.   Divine sanction was invoked for the institution with the Bible as evidence.   Historical precedent of the existence of slavery in every age was cited.   Culture, it was said, could thrive only if the few enjoyed leisure from exploitation of the many, and Negro slavery threw wide the door of opportunity to all white men by substituting race exploitation for class exploitation. Southern bond slavery was compared to Northern wage slavery to prove that the Negro slave shared more abundantly in the necessaries of life than the Northern wage earner.

Much of the abolitionists' reply to the Southern claims of cultural superiority and the defense of slavery as a humane and civilizing institution is to be found in the general indictments of slavery as a sin and as incompatible with the standards of contemporary civilization. They did not hesitate, however, to meet the argument on specific points, twitting the slaveholders about their lack of a common school system, their resort to murder under the *code duello* for the satisfaction of every fancied wrong, their compulsory diversion of all mixed blood back into the Negro race to hide the shame of their immorality, and their propensity for gambling and hard drinking. They ridiculed the idea that a system which made the happiness of a defenseless people "the sport of every whim, and the prey of every passion that may ... infest the master's bosom" could possibly develop a profound sense of responsibility in the slaveholder, holding that the "daily practice of forcibly robbing others and habitually living on the plunder can not but beget in the mind the *habit* of regarding the interests and happiness of those whom it robs, as of no sort of consequence in comparison with its own."[6] As for the slave, his very dependence impaired his manliness and independence of character, crushed his soul, and destroyed his ability to distinguish right from wrong. It cultivated immorality, placed a premium upon deception, and made lying and stealing acts of self-preservation.

The Bible argument waxed long and furiously, with perhaps a slight advantage to the abolitionists. Over the long view it appears to have been a rather fruitless discussion, without much influence one way or the other. Slavery's rôle in history was assessed as a liability rather than as a contribution to the glory and stability of Rome. It was condemned as an impediment to a balanced economy in the

[6] "Testimony of the Presbyterian Synod of Kentucky," *ibid.*, p. 61.

South, absorbing the capital necessary to industrial enterprise, denying the entrepreneur the public coöperation essential to the development of manufacturing, destroying the fertility of the soil through forced and incompetent labor, driving the non-slaveholder to the free states or ever farther back upon the margin of a bare subsistence level, turning the stream of foreign immigration elsewhere, and creating a contempt for manual labor on the part of the whites, the fruits of which were indolence on the one hand and arrogant snobbery on the other.

Finally, slavery was condemned as a menace to the peace and safety of the nation.  Concentration of Negroes in the Black Belt entered into every phase of the slavery question. From the earliest days the champions of slavery had admitted the necessity of maintaining a proper ratio between the two races.  The subject arose in connection with colonization. Southern pamphleteers conceded the desirability of diffusion as an aid to the alleviation of the system's harsher features. Fear of insurrection increased as the center of the slave population moved steadily toward the Southwest.  It was advanced in defense of the prohibition against teaching slaves to read, permitting them to assemble without the presence of whites, etc.  It played an important part in the discussion over the expansion of slave territory and in the Confederate Constitutional Convention with respect to the non-seceding states in 1861.

Abolitionists took particular delight, it would seem, in playing upon this fear of the South by exposing it as a national weakness, calling attention to the vulnerability of the southern coast to attack, chiding the South for dependence upon the great strength of the nation to protect from outside interference and from internal combustion an institution it insisted upon regarding as its own domestic concern, lashing out with bitter invective against the slavocracy for involving the whole nation in a war of conquest, and bringing all the pressure at their command against the state department's representations to Great Britain in the *Creole* and other cases.

The particular emphasis placed upon each of these several indictments depended upon the time, the occasion, and the person discussing the subject. It is essential to remember that the antislavery movement was almost completely unorganized until the founding of the American Anti-Slavery Society in December, 1833. There were the New York City Manumission Society, organized by John Jay and Alexander Hamilton in 1785; the Pennsylvania Abolition Society, organized by Benjamin Franklin in 1789; and scattered local societies in North Carolina, Tennessee, and southern Ohio; but the organized movement for the entire abolition of slavery in the United States began in the early thirties. From 1833 to 1840 it was under the direction of a powerful executive committee of the American Anti-Slavery Society, located in New York City. After 1839 there were two national organizations: the American Anti-Slavery Society, under the control of William Lloyd Garrison at Boston, and the American and Foreign Anti-Slavery Society, under the control of Lewis Tappan in New York City. During the first period work was carried on largely through local and traveling agents and was predominantly religious, with churches the forums, the sin of slavery the theme, and the organization of state and local auxiliary societies and the founding of antislavery newspapers an important function of the agents. After 1840 neither of the national organizations exercised much influence or control over the movement; but, so far as they did, the American and Foreign Anti-Slavery Society was the functional continuation of the original American Anti-Slavery Society, distinctly religious and friendly to the churches and promoting the old policy of seeking the abolition of slavery by moral suasion. The real work of maintaining agencies and newspapers and depositories for antislavery literature, how-

ever, was carried on by the powerful state societies. The
function of giving direction to the movement and defining
its objectives was now under the control of a small group of
politically minded abolitionists, and state societies shortly
became almost identical with state antislavery political parties.
The American Anti-Slavery Society under Garrison at Boston
—the old society name without the substance—was distinctly
antichurch, antipolitical, and strongly flavored with peace,
no-human-government, and woman's rights.

The sin of slavery and the Bible argument were first emphasized in the Lane Seminary debate and by the agents in
opening the churches and securing the support of the clergy.
Thenceforth noted theologians, North and South, published
elaborate treatises in the religious journals of the day; thousands of copies of sermons on the subject by such men as
John Rankin, Beriah Green, and Samuel Crothers, were distributed among the clergy; and a few books were circulated
by the hundred thousand, including Birney's *Letter to the
Ministers and Elders* (1834), Weld's *The Bible against
Slavery* (1837), and La Roy Sunderland's *The Testimony of
God against Slavery* (1835); but their influence was as nothing compared with the Bible quotations, usually accompa-
nied by appropriate etchings, impressed upon the letterheads
used by the officials of the societies or embroidered upon all
sorts of fancy work by the female abolitionists:

"Thou shalt not steal."

"Thou shalt love thy neighbor as thyself."

"All things whatsoever ye would that men should do to you, do
you even so to them."

"First, be reconciled to thy brother, and then come and offer thy
gift."

"He hath sent me to heal the broken-hearted, to preach deliverance
to the captives, to set at liberty them that are bruised."

"Woe unto him that buildeth his house by unrighteousness, and
his chambers by wrong; that useth his neighbor's service without wages,
and giveth him not for his work."

"And he that stealeth a man, and selleth him, or if he be found
in his hand, he shall surely be put to death."

"Open thy mouth for the dumb in the cause of all such as are appointed to destruction. Open thy mouth, judge righteously, and plead the cause of the poor and needy."

"This is my commandment, That ye love one another, as I have loved you."

This phase of the antislavery crusade is inseparable from the pioneering efforts of three Southern Presbyterian clergymen: George Bourne, whose book caused him to be convicted of heresy by the Virginia Synod and to be driven out of the state to the more friendly environment of Philadelphia; Samuel Doak, of Little Limestone, Tennessee, who sent one student after another into the ministry, with antislavery doctrines, in the region which later became the first battleground; and John Rankin, one of Doak's students, who carried the fight into one Presbyterian general assembly after another; but the organization of the movement on the principle of preaching the sin of slavery was Theodore Weld's great contribution, and it was the dominant note in antislavery effort while he retained direction of it, i.e. until 1840.

Weld and his wife, Angelina Grimké Weld, did more than anyone else to create the highly centralized picture of slavery as a barbaric institution. Their *American Slavery As It Is* was a complete anthology of horrors, and its sale probably equaled the combined sales of all other books of the sort before the publication of *Uncle Tom's Cabin*. It was published in 1839 and thenceforth there was no cessation of slave narratives, novels, etc., emphasizing one or another of slavery's sordid aspects.

Between 1834 and 1838 the challenge of slavery to civil rights in the North was made. Weld and the Lane Seminary boys who went out as agents met mob violence and overcame it by Christian meekness. Others, particularly the Cincinnati group of Levi Coffin, David Burnett, and William Birney, the Illinois group who defended Lovejoy's press, and the delegates to the first Ohio state convention, met violence with violence, and eventually forced the civil authorities to assume their responsibilities. It was Birney, however, who first saw the full significance of the denial of free enquiry and discussion, developed the thesis that slavery was incompatible with the fundamental principles of Americanism, and expanded the movement to free the Negro into a movement to preserve the essence of freedom for the white man. Edward Beecher, president of Illinois College, and Wendell Phillips of Boston were probably the two outstanding men induced to join the crusade by this contest over civil rights, and both were towers of strength. This broader aspect of the controversy will be the subject of our next lecture.

After 1840 the antislavery movement was political; the hustings were the forums; every candidate for office in an antislavery community was an antislavery lecturer; and the halls of Congress were the battleground. Myron Holley was the father of political action. Birney, Joshua Leavitt, and Alvan Stewart carried the burden after Holley's untimely death. The forties were the transition period, culminating in a Northern sectional party, but the central themes of the movement after 1840 were the withering influence of slavery upon the welfare and progress of the nation and the necessity of purging all branches of the federal government of its influence.

The scope of the abolition indictment of slavery, its widespread organization and skilful direction, and the length of time required to achieve its objective would seemingly indicate either a weak case or a strongly entrenched institution. Neither is correct. The weakness of the attack upon slavery and the strength of its defense lay not at all in one or the other per se, but in the fact that slavery was so inextricably bound up with the nation's political philosophy that the two were inseparable; and the indictment of slavery, because it was not allowed to operate upon the minds and hearts of the Southern people, embraced and came to be identified with a new political philosophy, unsupported by precedent or tradition and hostile to the genius of the people.

# IV. DEFENSE OF CIVIL RIGHTS

"TO PREACH distant reform is very cheap philanthropy, —the cheaper in proportion to the distance. The feeling of self-satisfaction exists without the necessity of personal sacrifice."[1] So wrote the South Carolinian, Julius Pringle, in 1852. Had he lived in the North during the years 1834–39, he would have been less inclined to regard the abolition of slavery as a distant reform and would have been more aware of the personal sacrifice involved in its advocacy. James G. Birney was not engaging in effusive rhetoric when he wrote to Gerrit Smith: "The antagonist principles of liberty and slavery have been roused into action and one or the other must be victorious. There will be no cessation of the strife, until Slavery shall be exterminated or liberty destroyed."[2] He was saying the same thing that Seward and Lincoln said in their "Irrepressible Conflict" and "House Divided" speeches twenty-five years later. The essential difference is that the two latter men failed to discern the danger until the crisis was past and the victory won. Their speeches caught the attention of historians whose eyes have been focused upon the election of 1860, and the more important period from 1834 to 1844, together with the men who then bore the battle, has remained in obscurity. Freedom was on the defensive, and an abolitionist was an object of scorn, even of bitter hatred, in 1834. *Slavery* was on the defensive, and an abolitionist was elected to the presidency in 1860. The difference represents the change of a generation in public opinion in the North.

[1] [Pringle, Julius], *Slavery in the Southern States* (Cambridge, 1852), p. 3.
[2] James G. Birney to Gerrit Smith, September 13, 1835, *Birney Letters*, I, 343.

Slavery as an economic system was of small account compared with slavery as a system of racial adjustment and social control. In its broader aspects slavery was the apotheosis of the principle of Negro inferiority, a functional philosophy which overreached the geographical limits of bond labor and conditioned social attitudes. The outward manifestation of such a functional philosophy at any given time is called public opinion. So we are accustomed to speak of public opinion as influencing our legislative bodies, our executive officers, and even our judiciary. It is only a partially correct observation. Changes in the basic philosophy of a people are as imperceptible but fully as irresistible as the ebb and flow of the tides. Institutional changes—constitutions and constitutional interpretations, religious doctrines, political alignments, and governmental policies—follow with equal certainty and precision. Public opinion rises, falls, and changes its course with the fitfulness of the winds, ever sensitive to fortuitous circumstances and the vagaries of the hour. It is indicative of the direction, though not of the degree, of a changing philosophy, and the intellectual ferment produced by its tornadic disturbances leaves an indelible impression upon that philosophy. The lag gives stability to our institutions and pain to our reformers.

Belief in the biological inequality and the racial inferiority of the Negro not only sustained slavery and colonization, but also determined the attitude of the public, the zeal of law-enforcement officials, the reasoning of judicial bodies, the efficiency of administrative functionaries, and the definition of policies by legislatures and Congress in all matters pertaining to Negroes and abolitionists. Slavery was not the source of the philosophy. It merely enshrined it, prevented a practical demonstration of its falsity, and filled public offices and the councils of religious, educational, and political institutions with men reared in its atmosphere. So long as the temple stood, men clung to the faith. Bond or free, the

Negro found it "paralyzing to enterprise, destructive to ambition, ruinous to character, crushing to mind,"[3] and the vigilant white could not ignore its subversive threat to the rights of free men.

The denial of freedom of the press at Danville and of academic freedom at Lane Seminary, the first by mob violence, the second by faculty decree, were but the prelude to riots of mob violence unequalled in any other period in the nation's history. The worst offenses were in the border free states, particularly Illinois, Ohio, Pennsylvania, and New York, strongholds of colonization contiguous to the slave states and havens of refuge for fugitive slaves. The Lane Seminary rebels bore the brunt of the violence against antislavery lecturers, partly because they were pioneers, partly because the faculty disseminated the idea that they were monomaniacs and disturbers of the peace. They dared not venture into the slave states. Standing upon the banks of the Ohio, about to cross over into Kentucky from whose dangers he had been warned by his sister, a seventeen-year-old member of the band wrote: "I have had great change of circumstances, since I became an Abolitionist. Before I had money as I wanted. My father was a man of influence and as his son I was respected and loved by all who knew me both in Kentucky and here. Now the people of Kentucky would shun me as they would a rattle-snake. And the nobility of Marietta are as cool towards me as can be."[4]

Birney was cautioned against crossing the river. Writing to him on August 3, 1836, his sister said: "You seem to be hunted like the hare. Pray let not the similitude be kept up—do not be found in the lair from whence you were started";[5]

[3] Work, Monroe N., "The Life of Charles B. Ray," *Journal of Negro History,* IV, 361–362.

[4] James W. Davis to Theodore D. Weld, February 22, 1836, *Weld–Grimké Letters,* I, 266.

[5] Anna R. Marshall to James G. Birney, August 3, 1836, *Birney Letters,* I, 348.

and, as late as 1839, his father warned: "You must not think of entering Kentucky—danger would lurk in every step you took here—even Arthur Tappan would be as safe here as you. . . . I implore you if you wish to see me I will if I am able go to Cincinnati."[6]  It became almost impossible to liquidate his estate in Alabama, since he was forced to rely upon the services of an incompetent attorney, his former law partner finding some excuse to decline his account.

The Reverend David Nelson printed and distributed a farewell admonition to his parishioners at Danville, Kentucky, and addressed it also to his new congregation at Marion, Missouri, on the text: "Thou shalt not covet thy neighbor's time; thou shalt not covet thy neighbor's toil; nor his sweat; nor his bones; nor his blood; nor his soul; nor any thing that is thy neighbor's."  He denounced slavery as a sin "blacker and more horrible" than intemperance, and prophesied: "That bell of warning will be hammered on, whether postmasters are willing or not.  Abolitionists were slaveholders or indifferent spectators only *yesterday*.  They have not at all times, I think, spoken with becoming Charity.  I ask forgiveness for all unthinking harshness, but God forbid that I should ever again be silent."[7]  Scarcely had he entered upon his duties at Palmyra, seat of Marion College, when his services were interrupted by a bloody riot between slaveholders and gradual emancipationists.  Nelson's only offense was reading from the pulpit the offer of one of his congregation to contribute $10,000 for compensated emancipation.  Leaving his property behind, Nelson was hurried to safety beyond the Mississippi, but returned to sit at the bedside of a son ill of the fever.  It was while he was on the emergency mission of paternal devotion that ninety of the leading citizens delivered to him an ultimatum to leave the county immediately and

[6] *Birney Letters,* I, 347 n.

[7] Nelson, David, *Last Advice to My Old and Beloved Congregation at Danville, Kentucky* (no date or publisher given).

forever or "receive such treatment as the feelings of an outraged community may dictate."[8]  The faculty of Marion College passed resolutions forbidding the students to circulate abolition literature, to converse with slaves, or to discuss the subject of slavery under any circumstances.

At St. Louis a mob removed from jail a Negro charged with homicide and burned him at the stake.  Judge Lawless instructed the Grand Jury to act against the participants only if preliminary investigation revealed that a "few" men rather than "many" men were involved.  The Reverend Elijah P. Lovejoy, editor of the *St. Louis Observer*, ventured to criticize the whole unsavory incident, only to have his establishment demolished and himself exiled, under penalty of death.  He removed to Alton, Illinois, where he set up the *Alton Observer*, and joined with the Reverend David Nelson, Gideon Blackburn, Edward Beecher, and others in forming the Illinois Anti-Slavery Society.  The organization meeting was invaded by the opponents of free inquiry.  Colonizationists hurled bitter invectives at everyone connected with the movement.  Three times the presses were destroyed and, in defense of the fourth, Lovejoy was killed.

Chance alone saved Birney from a similar fate at Cincinnati.  The *Philanthropist* had been established finally at Cincinnati in January, 1836, but until April the actual publishing was done at New Richmond twenty miles north. A mob invaded the printing office during the night of July 12 and wrecked the type.  The mayor, S. W. Davies, warned the Ohio State Anti-Slavery Society, whose organ the *Philanthropist* was, to cease its publication.  A great public meeting was held in the Lower Market House, presided over by Postmaster William Burke, at which resolutions were passed eulogizing as comparable to the patriots of the Boston Tea Party any who should resort to similar methods against abolitionists.  A committee was appointed to remonstrate with the

[8] *Quarterly Anti-Slavery Magazine*, II, No. 4 (July, 1837), p. 397.

publisher, including in its membership Jacob Burnet, former Ohio state supreme court judge and United States senator; Josiah Lawrence and Robert Buchanan, presidents of the city's largest banks; Nicholas Longworth, largest property holder in the city; and David T. Disney, former speaker of the Ohio House of Representatives. This committee warned Birney of a mob "unusual in its number, determined in its purpose, and desolating in its ravages," and refused to countenance the continued publication of the *Philanthropist,* even though ways could be found to avert mob violence, thus identifying themselves with its sponsors. The mob was assembled on the night of July 30, the press was thrown into the Ohio River, homes of the city's Negro section were invaded and their inmates subjected to all sorts of abuses, and the mob dispersed only after the mayor admonished them of the lateness of the hour and the danger, unless they retired, of disturbing the respectable citizens and depriving them of their rest. Birney was absent from the city. Returning early the following morning, he was met at the outskirts and hurried to safety by his friends. He refused to leave the city, but weeks elapsed before he could walk safely on the streets even in daylight.

Antislavery lecturers were mobbed wherever they put in their appearance and were recognized. Weld was refused permission to lecture in the Presbyterian and Episcopal churches at Circleville, Ohio, and forced to use an empty room in a store. On March 2, 1835, he wrote: "Stones and clubs flew merrily against the shutters. At the close as I came out, curses were showered in profusion. Lamp black, nails, divers pockets full of stones and eggs had been provided for the occasion, and many had disguised their persons, smeared their faces, etc., to avoid recognition. . . . Next evening same state of things, with increase of violent demonstrations. The next, such was the uproar that a number of gentlemen insisted upon forming an escort and seeing me safe to my lodging, which they did. This state of things lasted till I had lectured six or seven times, then hushed down and for the latter part of the course had a smooth sea."[9]

At Willoughby the Methodist minister declared that he would stand in the door of his church with a club to keep James A. Thome and John W. Alvord from lecturing, so they moved on to Middlebury, from which place Alvord wrote, on February 9, 1836: "Last evening Middlebury puked. . . . Spasmodic heavings and retchings were manifest during the whole day. . . . All [was] still until about 8 [o'clock] when in came a broadside of Eggs. Glass, Egg shells, whites and yolks flew on every side. Br. Thome's Fact Book received an egg just in its bowels, and I doubt whether one in the House escaped a spattering. I have been trying to clean off this morning, but can't get off the stink. Thome dodged like a stoned gander. He brought up at length against the side of the desk, cocked his eye and stood gazing upward at the flying missels as they streamed in ropy masses through the house. . . . The mob threaten today dreadfully. . . . There are a few determined men here, but the mob are set on by men of influence most of whom are church members. Abolitionists heretofore in this place have always been mobbed out. We must try to carry the day this time if possible."[10]

At Zanesville Weld could not secure so much as a shanty in which to lecture. At Putnam he was mobbed, and every kind of outrage was committed against the Negroes as a consequence of his inviting them to attend his lectures. They were turned out of employment, men were prosecuted under the vandal laws for employing them, and the entire population was thrown into a frenzy of fear as houses were torn down in profusion. A Negro appeared shortly afterward as a delegate to the antislavery convention, but a committee of the

[9] Theodore D. Weld to Elizur Wright, Jr., March 2, 1835, *Weld–Grimké Letters*, I, 207.

[10] James A. Thome and John W. Alvord to Theodore D. Weld, February 9, 1836, *ibid.*, pp. 360–361.

Negro population came to Weld in agony and terror, begging that no Negroes be allowed to enter the convention for fear of their own lives and the vengeance of the mob upon the colored people of the community.

The Ohio Anti-Slavery Convention of 1836 was held at Granville. With prophecies of certain death by mob violence, every tavern keeper within a radius of twenty miles sought to discourage delegates from attending. A schoolhouse in which Thome attempted to lecture two miles south of Granville was almost totally destroyed. Four express coaches were sent to St. Albans, Mount Vernon, and Newark by the most respectable citizens of the town to bring in ruffians from those points. A bloody battle ensued in which numerous casualties were inflicted, and finally the delegates to the convention rode away on their horses amid a shower of eggs and curses without a single prominent citizen willing to utter a protest.

Were one to recount the details of every mobbing of antislavery lecturers, it would require volumes. Henry B. Stanton was mobbed one hundred and fifty times before 1840, and Theodore D. Weld could be traced from one end of the country to the other by such outbursts. They were as much a part of his daily routine as eating his breakfast.

Occasionally mob violence assumed the character of a general riot, in which neither human life nor property was spared. Lewis Tappan's home in New York was plundered, his furniture broken up, carried into the street and burned. His store, the home and church of the Reverend A. L. Cox, the church of the Reverend H. G. Ludlow, three Negro churches, a Negro school, and twenty Negro homes were badly damaged at the same time. Pennsylvania Hall in Philadelphia, built by subscription at a cost of $40,000, was opened May 14, 1838, and dedicated by extensive ceremonies. Two days later the Female Anti-Slavery Convention which assembled there was invaded and the building burned to the ground. An academy, built by subscription in Canaan, New Hampshire, and chartered by the state in 1834, was dragged from its foundation by one hundred oxen, August 10, 1835, because fourteen of the forty-two pupils were Negroes. Rioting broke out in Philadelphia in August, 1834, and continued for three days, during which a Negro amusement house, a Negro Presbyterian church, and forty-five Negro houses were destroyed. This riot was known as "the Passover Riot" because whites living in the same sections placed lights in their windows to distinguish them from the Negro homes. In Pittsburgh, in 1839, a Negro procession celebrating emancipation in the West Indies was broken up, many Negroes were injured, and both the African Hall and the Presbyterian Church were set on fire.

Was there no connection between rearing children to be sold in the market place and this denial of human rights so proudly proclaimed in the Declaration of Independence and the preamble of the Constitution? Look at the record: the dignified and brilliant James G. Birney, sired and reared in the Kentucky Bluegrass, blood relation and confidant of the oldest families of the South, driven from his native state, mobbed and hunted like a dog in the streets of Cincinnati, his newspaper press destroyed and his family kept in constant apprehension of violent death; Elijah P. Lovejoy, the lowly publisher of St. Louis, driven from the city, followed up to Alton and killed; the venerable David Nelson, distinguished minister and educator, driven from Marion College, to seek safety at Carlinville, and hunted for days by a drunken rabble of armed men as he lay concealed in the forest with his little children; Pennsylvania Hall, a monument to free speech and an edifice of architectural beauty, burned to the ground because someone dared to raise his voice there against the system of human bondage; one hundred and thirty young men forced to leave Lane Seminary because they challenged the prevailing belief in Negro inferiority; Prudence Crandall's school in

New England torn from its foundations because she admitted a mulatto girl; even in New York the churches and homes of those who extended a helping hand to the despised and under-privileged subjected to destruction. All these things, and more, with a knowledge of, and ofttimes in the presence of, public officials whose sworn duty it was to uphold the law, in the presence of courts established and maintained to dispense justice, and under the eyes of governors and legislators who had ceased to reverence the majesty of the law.

The right of the individual to inquire into all subjects and to communicate freely his thoughts and opinions to others by word of mouth or through the press and the right of everyone to the protection of person and property were fundamental principles of the nation's birth. It is almost superfluous to say that the right of free discussion is not dependent upon the exercise of prudence or wisdom. Indiscretion does not abrogate the right. It may be curtailed only for abuse, only by law, and only after determination of abuse in the courts. It is the heartbeat of the democratic process, the golden specific of human progress. When civil authorities fail to extend protection to persons and property, anarchy reigns. In the words of Edward Beecher, "when law is prostrate, a nation is slain."

These principles were trampled under foot because people of intelligence and power were so divided on the question of slavery that their moral influence in their communities was neutralized. Men allowed their hatred of abolition doctrine to weaken their reverence for the majesty of the law. They forgot that principles of free inquiry and protection, to be secure, must be sustained independently of the opinions expressed and of the persons requiring protection. They allowed the will of the majority to become the criterion of right and wrong, and mob violence to undermine the foundations of civil government.

Slavery and free discussion were incompatible, but the attempt to suppress the latter served mightily to hasten the former's destruction.   Said Elijah Lovejoy, standing in the shadow of death: "You have courts, and judges and juries; they find nothing against me.   And now you come together for the purpose of driving out a confessedly innocent man, for no cause but that he dares to think and speak as his conscience and his God dictate.   Will conduct like this stand the scrutiny of your country? of posterity?   Above all, of the judgment-day? . . .   You may hang me up as the mob hung up the individuals of Vicksburg.   You may burn me at the stake, as they did McIntosh at St. Louis; or, you may tar and feather me, or throw me into the Mississippi, as you have often threatened to do; but you can not disgrace me. . . .   I dare not flee away from Alton.   Should I attempt it, I should feel that the angel of the Lord with his flaming sword was pursuing me wherever I went . . . the contest has commenced here, and here it must be finished. . . .   If I fall, my grave shall be made in Alton."[11]   He fell that night, where today a monument stands, erected to his memory by a great commonwealth whose civil authorities refused to save his life.   No more accurate history was ever written after an event than the prophecy of his biographer: "Ten thousand presses had he employed them all, could never have done what the simple tale of his death will do.   Up and down the mighty streams of the West his voice will go; it will penetrate the remotest corner of our land; it will be heard to the extremities of the civilized world. From henceforth no boat will pass the spot where he fell, heedless of his name, or of his sentiments, or of the cause for which he died."[12]

Congress and the courts were no less slaves to the prevailing philosophy than the drunken rabble of Alton, Illinois, had been.   Of greater historical importance than the denial

[11] Beecher, Edward, *Narrative of Riots at Alton, in Connection with the Death of Reverend Elijah P. Lovejoy* (Alton, 1838), pp. 89–91.

[12] *Ibid.*, p. 102.

of free speech, free press, and the protection of persons and property to abolitionists was the denial to the Negro of protection of his status as a free man.    Abuse of abolitionists resulted from a collapse of the orderly processes of government in a local community.    The recession was temporary, lasting only a few years and, in most communities, only a few months. At the worst, the abolitionist might lose his property, receive a coat of tar and feathers, be bruised about; but he seldom lost his life, nor was he silenced for long.    The Negro, on the contrary, was in constant danger of being seized and sold down the river to a living death, and the full power of a state government was insufficient to prevent it.

The Constitution of the United States provided that "No person held to service or labor in one State, under the laws thereof, escaping into another, shall, in consequence of any law or regulation therein, be discharged from such service or labor, but shall be delivered up on claim of the party to whom such service or labor may be due."[13]    The law of 1793, for the rendition of fugitives from justice and of fugitive slaves, gave power to arrest to the claimant or his agent.    Oral or written testimony had then to be presented to any judicial officer of the federal, state, or local governments.    Such magistrate was empowered to issue a certificate of transfer to the claimant's state.

Leaving the question of the constitutionality of the act for later consideration, and stripping of extraneous material the law, the procedure provided for, and the court decisions arising from its enforcement, we are confronted with these simple facts, not one of which is open to successful refutation:

(1) Neither the Constitution nor the act of 1793 made any mention of Negroes or white men.    The terms used were "person held to labor" and "person to whom such labor or service may be due."    So far as the language of the act itself was concerned, there was not the slightest evidence that it applied to Negroes and not to white men, and no reason for be-

[13] Article IV, Section II, Paragraph 3.

lieving that it would not have been applicable in case some state had held in bondage Mexicans or Indians or even white men with red hair.

(2) Every slaveholder or slaveholders' agent in the United States was clothed with authority by this act to go into any free state and seize any Negro, irrespective of whether he was a fugitive slave, had purchased his freedom, had been manumitted, or had lived in the community all his life and had never seen a slave state.

(3) Not until after the seizure must the arresting party seek a court of justice, usually a local justice of the peace, and present testimony, written or oral, of his right to ownership of the Negro.

(4) The justice, at his own discretion, then made the decision which restored the Negro to freedom or sent him off to an eternity of servitude. There was no provision for testimony in his own behalf by the Negro or for calling of witnesses or for jury trial, or for delay to permit investigation of the evidence; there were no extenuating circumstances such as marriage, ownership of property, long period of residence, etc.; no safeguards, in fact, against kidnaping. No Negro was secure, and homes of Negroes and whites alike could be and were invaded in the search for lost property.

(5) State laws to protect the free Negro by requiring the claimant to obtain a warrant for the arrest or requiring trial by jury were invalidated by the Supreme Court. Congress was held to have exclusive jurisdiction, and the prompt, certain return of the fugitive, with the least possible cost or annoyance to the owner, was considered paramount to protection of the free Negro against enslavement. The philosophy of the Court was the philosophy of slavery, that a Negro was presumed to be a slave, rather than the philosophy of freedom, that every man was presumed to be free unless proved to be a slave.

It is essential to remember that we are speaking of the period of the thirties. Slowly the philosophy of the Northern people changed as the antislavery movement prospered. Harsh provisions of the "black codes" were eliminated, mob violence against abolitionists and free Negroes occurred less frequently, local and then state governments felt the influence of the movement.    The local magistrate became less likely to issue a certificate for the removal of a Negro without strong evidence that he was a fugitive.    Public sentiment made it as dangerous for the slave-catcher to venture into many communities as it had been for the abolitionists a few years earlier, and it was precisely through such communities that the underground railroad moved the fugitives to Canada or its southern border.

The vast network of antislavery societies throughout the Northern states was now an integral part of the political pattern.    Men seeking public office could no longer ignore the votes of antislavery constituents, the power of antislavery newspapers, the direct challenge of preëlection antislavery questionnaires.    Abolitionists constituted a powerful pressure group in a constantly increasing number of Northern communities.    They captured control of the local offices, particularly the school boards, the justices of peace, the sheriffs, and the county courts.    Their influence was felt in the state governments.    Connecticut, Massachusetts, New York, Vermont, and Pennsylvania attempted to prevent kidnaping by requiring the claimant to obtain a warrant for the arrest of a fugitive or by requiring trial by jury in fugitive slave cases.    Then came the decision of the Supreme Court in the case of *Prigg* v. *Pennsylvania* (1842), a decision which, in historical importance, far outweighed the Dred Scott decision of 1857, because it invalidated all efforts of the Northern states to protect the civil rights and the liberties of an important class of persons under their jurisdiction by legislation designed to supplement and supply the deficiencies of the federal act of 1793 in that respect.

The Prigg decision held that Congressional power over the subject of fugitive slaves was exclusive, thus furnishing ample justification, had the sectional controversy been confined to this single question alone, for the antislavery effort to gain control of the federal government. Meanwhile, however, in the majority opinion (Taney dissenting) the Court had said that, so far as the act of 1793 conferred authority upon state magistrates, it was valid; that such magistrates might exercise the authority unless prohibited by state legislation; but that the states might constitutionally prohibit their magistrates from acting. It was this part of the decision which partially quieted abolition protests and inspired Justice Story to speak of the decision as "a triumph of freedom." Northern states revised their statutes to prohibit state officials from participating in the enforcement of the federal statute. Congress retaliated with the Fugitive Slave Act of 1850 providing that commissioners should be appointed by the circuit courts to carry out the provisions of the act and were to have concurrent jurisdiction with the judges of the circuit and district courts; that fugitives were to be reclaimed for the owners or their agent by warrant issued by these commissioners; that, in case of trial, the Court was to hear the evidence and grant a certificate to the owner for the removal of the fugitive from the state; and that the fee of the commissioner for deciding in favor of the claimant was to be ten dollars, and against the claimant, five dollars.

The storm of protest which followed passage of this act never subsided. State after state passed so-called personal liberty laws, many of them clearly nullifying the provisions of the federal statute, guaranteeing to fugitives the writ of habeas corpus and trial by jury, prohibiting the use of all state and county jails for the detention of alleged fugitives, imposing heavy penalties for kidnaping, obliging state attorneys to defend alleged fugitives at state expense, imposing heavy fines upon any citizen or public official who assisted in the enforcement of the federal act, and granting freedom to all slaves brought within the state. It is important here to keep in mind the clear distinction between a state failing to pass legislation in support of a federal statute or forbidding its officials to enforce a federal statute and a state passing legislation in direct contravention of a federal statute. The federal government is obliged to enforce its own laws, and no state is constitutionally obliged to lend its assistance, though it has often been claimed that a moral obligation to do so exists. State legislation contravening federal legislation has, however, no constitutional effect, though actually it has often been considered of great value as a safety valve at times of great public excitement. Some of the personal liberty laws belong in each of these categories.

The Fugitive Slave Act of 1850 was clearly designed, like the act of 1793, to facilitate the return of fugitives without regard to the security of free men. Unlike the earlier act, which did not require admission of testimony of the fugitive, this act specifically forbade it. What further evidence could be presented that the mental processes of the congress which passed or the court which sustained a statute denying a person claimed as a slave the poor privilege of refuting the claim were perverted by the fact that those affected were Negroes rather than whites? Slaves were property, but not all Negroes were slaves, and, so long as these acts remained on the statute books, the rights of free men were in jeopardy.

Finally, there was the question of the right of petition, first placed under discussion in 1835. From January 28, 1840, to December, 1844, the House of Representatives operated under a standing rule: "That no petition, memorial, resolution, or other paper praying the abolition of slavery in the District of Columbia, or any State or Territory, or the slave trade between the States or Territories of the United States in which it now exists, shall be received by this House, or entertained in any way whatever." The rule was intended by its sponsor to be and was regarded by the antislavery men as an attempt to suppress discussion of the slavery question. It was a denial of the right of petition and a threat to democratic government.

# V. SLAVERY AND THE CONSTITUTION

W E HAVE been discussing, up to this time, the several steps in the development of a sectional alignment on the question of slavery: (1) emancipation in all the Northern states; retention and strengthening of slavery in all the Southern states; (2) migration of many antislavery men and women from the slave states to the free states; (3) withdrawal of antislavery men from the colonization society and organization of militant antislavery societies. We have analyzed the abolition indictment of slavery, and the Southern defense of it as a positive good; and explained how this controversy ceased to be one of slavery or freedom for the Negro alone and broadened out into a challenge and defense of the civil rights of free men. Having done this, we must now determine how and why slavery became a political question of national import. Let me repeat that the philosophies of the two contending sectional parties in 1860 grew out of the early phases of the slavery controversy and developed concurrently with the trend toward sectionalism; that these political philosophies were perfectly designed to accomplish the respective sectional aims of securing complete emancipation on the one hand and absolute security for slavery on the other; and that on the day these two sectional parties sought control of the federal government sectionalism was complete, the question of slavery and the question of governmental structure were synchronized, and a dual revolution was in progress.

We must now turn our attention to an analysis of these constitutional interpretations of the proslavery and the antislavery groups, the origin of a Northern sectional party, and its avowed purpose with respect to governmental policies. Incidental reference to the origin of the Southern sectional party will be necessary, though of less importance because its philosophy had long been dominant in both of the old party caucuses and consequently in the shaping of governmental policies.

In order to be readily intelligible, the constitutional argument with respect to slavery must be discussed under three headings, although they are not wholly separable: (1) the intentions of the founding fathers with respect to slavery and the moral obligations of the states and of individuals to carry out those intentions; (2) the extent and nature of the powers conferred upon Congress; and (3) the nature of government. The first embraces the higher-law doctrine; the second, the compact theory of the Constitution; and the third, the doctrine of concurrent majority.

On December 27, 1837, John C. Calhoun introduced into the Senate a series of resolutions epitomizing the philosophy of slavery with respect to the invisible bonds of Union. Like the doctrine of concurrent majority, with which we shall deal later, they rested upon the state rights thesis, but dealt principally with the purpose of union and the rights and obligations of both states and federal government arising out of it. The several states, said Calhoun, formed the Union to increase their security against both foreign and domestic dangers, and to enhance the enjoyment of their "natural, political and social" advantages. They did not delegate to the general government but retained, each to itself, control over their domestic institutions, and "any intermeddling of any one or more States, or a combination of their citizens, with the domestic institutions and policy of the others, on any ground or under any pretext whatever, political, moral, or religious, with the view to their alteration, or subversion, is an assumption of superiority not warranted by the Constitution; insulting to the States interfered with, tending to endanger their domestic peace and tranquillity, subversive of the objects for which the Constitution was formed, and, by necessary consequence, tending to weaken and destroy the Union itself." The federal government, in fulfillment of its obligation to promote the "mutual security and prosperity" of the several states, was duty-bound to use its powers to uphold and strengthen the domestic institutions of the states, and to resist all effort of one section to convert it from an instrument of defense into an instrument of attack upon the domestic institutions of another section. Slavery existed in the southern and western states, as "an important part of their domestic institutions," previous to the adoption of the Constitution. It was recognized as such by the Constitution, and attacks upon it by the citizens of other states, because of a change in feeling, were not only unjustified, but were a violation of the terms of the compact and of "the most solemn obligations, moral and religious." Agitation for the abolition of slavery in the District of Columbia or in any of the territories, and any action by Congress to that effect, would be a "direct and dangerous attack on the institutions of all the slaveholding States." Any attempt to exclude slavery from any territory or state which might be acquired, on the grounds that it was "immoral or sinful, or otherwise obnoxious," would destroy the equality of the states, an equivalent to the destruction of the Union.[1]

This was not only Calhoun's personal opinion; it was the philosophy of slaveholders. It annihilated any notion that the South was not responsible for the attempt to put down discussion in the North and goes far to explain the intensity of the struggle for free inquiry. It designated the institution of slavery as a holy of holies against which no man within the confines of the United States might raise his voice. It denied the right of an individual or of a state to urge upon Congress the exclusion of slavery from the District of Columbia or the territories and of Congress to do aught but strengthen, defend, and extend it. It demanded the use of the full power of the government to suppress agitation against it. Why? Because

---

[1] *Cong. Globe,* 25 Cong., 2 Sess., 55.

slavery was a domestic institution of the South and existed at the time of the adoption of the Constitution, and to question its righteousness was to violate the terms of the original compact and the moral obligations assumed by the founding fathers and their descendants forever.

The higher-law doctrine of the abolitionists was a direct refutation of every item in this constitutional interpretation. It must be considered in relation (1) to the right of free inquiry, (2) to the institution of slavery, and (3) to the Constitution.

Man, said the abolitionists, is a free moral agent, endowed with inalienable rights as an individual by the creative act of God. The right of the individual to inquire freely into all subjects and to communicate freely his ideas to others is God's indispensable medium of regeneration, his instrument for renovating the world. It is the right of the individual to know God's will and his duty to execute it. He must be free from restraint to do it, free to contemplate the sublime thoughts of all ages, free to engage in contemporary discussion of principles of right conduct, free to anticipate posterity's judgments on moral questions, free to exercise all his influence in directing aright the slow-moving current of human destiny. These rights and duties, arising out of the nature of the human mind and the relationship between God and man, were indestructible by human government, superior to the Constitution, indelible by the surging waves of public opinion.

Cessation of antislavery agitation was, therefore, impossible. "The great current of human destiny bore this subject onward as one of the great practical questions of the age. On it the intellect of the civilized world was aroused; and to it the Spirit of God gave a resistless course."[2] Legal recognition of a property right in slaves did not alter the fact that

---

[2] Beecher, Edward, *Narrative of Riots at Alton, in Connection with the Death of Reverend Elijah P. Lovejoy* (Alton, 1838), p. 17.

they were human beings. The system of slavery authorized and, in its very nature, assured "the destruction of all rights of knowledge, of conscience, of marriage and family, of chastity, of property, of reputation and influence, and of protection against personal abuse."[3] It was incompatible with God's plan and contrary to the manifest destiny of the human race, unmistakably so in view of its existence "in the very focal point of illumination for the world on the great subject of inalienable rights." It could not possibly survive under God's providence unless He intended "to roll back the wheels of time, and plunge the nations in a second night of ages."[4] No man, therefore, who sought to do the will of God, could abandon the cause. "The deepest of all disgrace," said Love-joy, "would be, at a time like this, to deny my Master by for-saking his Cause."[5]

Finally (and it seems to me that here was the more important part of the higher-law doctrine), there was the specific point of constitutional interpretation. Abolitionists had, from the first, insisted that slavery not only was morally wrong, but was contrary to the principles on which the nation was established; that there were laws, consisting of rules of right, existing in the public mind prior to the establishment of the Constitution, by which even the framers of the Constitution and all subsequent legislative bodies were bound; that the Declaration of Independence was as binding in this country as the Magna Charta and Bill of Rights in Great Britain; and that slavery was repugnant to the principles of liberty published to the world in the Declaration of Independence, principles which constituted an "atmospheric medium" under the influence of which every part of the political machine was to be propelled.

The truths set forth in the Declaration of Independence, it was said, had been known previous to that time, and had been practiced by many individuals, but had never before

[3] *Ibid.,* p. 115.      [4] *Ibid.*      [5] *Ibid.,* p. 90.

been made the basis of government.    Previously governments
had been controlled by aristocracies of one type or another,
for selfish purposes and to the neglect of the masses, whose
happiness was a matter of indifference to government and
whose activities were "confined to strictly manual and brutish
occupations."    We had established the principle that a man's
ability, and not his condition of birth or class, should determine his place in society and in public esteem; and had provided "the means and the incentive for elevating the great
mass of the community."    "When, therefore," said Birney,
"in the midst of a struggle for political independence, it was
announced, that all men are created equal; that they are endowed by their Creator with the right of life, liberty and the
pursuit of happiness—and that, therefore, these endowments
are inalienable; that governments are instituted to secure
*them;* that governments exist only by the consent of the governed; that the people, whenever they choose, may properly
put them down and reconstruct them on better principles;—
when these were announced as the substratum of the new government, without alienating from us any who might have been
actuated in our behalf by other and lower motives, it at once
secured us the good will and the good wishes of all benevolent
and deep-thinking men."[6]

This association of ideas and regulative principles in the
Declaration advertised to other nations and to individuals the
nature of the new government, and we were in honor bound
as a people never to do anything woefully contrary to that
profession of faith.    The Declaration having defined the nature of government, the Constitution then defined the relationship between the government and the individual.    If
the Constitution recognized the institution of slavery and provided for its protection, continuance, and extension, in short,
if the constitutional interpretation of the slaveholders was cor-

[6] Birney, James G., "*Prigg* vs. *Pennsylvania.*"    Unpublished manu-
script.

rect, then the Constitution and the Declaration of Independence were irreconcilable. The same generation of men, in fact, many of the same individuals who had signed the Declaration, had lived through the Revolutionary period and had framed the Constitution. To suppose, said Birney, "before the dust and sweat of the Revolution was well wiped away from those men, that they would falsify the principles for which they risked their lives, in consenting to fasten slavery *forever* on the weakest of their fellow creatures—on man—woman—child—and even the infant yet unborn—is what I will not do, except on testimony that cannot be overthrown —testimony that I have never yet seen or heard."[7]

In support of this thesis that the Declaration of Independence was a functional part of the nation's fundamental law, that the Constitution could never have been intended to be a proslavery document, because slavery was incompatible with the principles enunciated in the Declaration, and that the generation which launched the new nation expected slavery to be speedily abolished, the abolitionists traced the course of governmental policy with respect to slavery during the early years of the Republic:

(1) Benjamin Franklin, who was president of the Pennsylvania Society for Promoting Abolition of Slavery, had presented a petition to the first Congress strongly urging it to use the full limits of its powers to free the slaves. James Wilson, Thomas Dawes, and others had assured their state ratifying conventions that there would be no more slave states. The Virginia delegation to the Constitutional Convention, made up of slaveholders, had endorsed the expectation of slavery's early extinction. The Georgia and South Carolina delegates alone had been recalcitrant. All the New England and Middle States had emancipated their slaves or were in process of doing so when the Convention met. Not only was their approval of the new instrument of government as essential as

[7] *Ibid.*

that of the slave states, but, viewing the progress of emancipation, the Convention might well have anticipated "that Justice and Humanity, now starting forth with fresh vigor, would, in their march, sweep away the whole system; more especially, as freedom of speech and of the press—the legitimate abolisher not only of the acknowledged vice of slavery, but of every other that time should reveal in our institutions or practices—had been fully secured to the people."[8]    Slaves and slavery were not mentioned in the Constitution, so that one ignorant of conditions in the United States at that time would be unaware of the existence of the system from a reading of the document.    Certainly men intending to perpetuate an institution would have said so and not left it to inference.    The Ordinance of 1787 was designed to exclude slavery from all the territory then under control of the United States government and implied an intention to restrict it to existing states.

(2) The Convention, unwilling to lose the support of a single state, confidently expecting slavery to disappear at an early date, and desirous of providing for the highest degree of comity and good will, had agreed to the rendition of fugitive slaves and the introduction of foreign slaves for a period of years, except where prohibited by state law.    Slavery was recognized as an irreconcilable incident to the main purpose of the Union as expressed in the preamble of the Constitution, and the framers, finding it impossible to overcome all the difficulties in the way of its immediate overthrow, had expected the people of the remaining slave states and everyone vested with authority to move in the direction of its extinction at the earliest practicable moment.    Especially was it the duty of the several departments of the federal government—the Supreme Court, Congress, and the president—in every case where a doubtful decision had to be made, to decide "in favor of liberty and against what restrains it . . . not to weaken

[8] Birney, *op. cit.*

the main purpose of the government . . . and give permanency, life and weight to the inconsistent incident."[9]

(3) These expectations had been frustrated with the passing of time. The critical period came to an end with complete acknowledgment of our independent status, and we grew in stature as a people with an expanding commerce and national prestige. Forgetful of the principles which, in the hour of our distress, had been used to justify our stroke for independence, we had succumbed to the power of wealth gleaned from exploitation of the weakest among us. Not only had the slaveholding states failed to live up to expectations in the matter of emancipation, but, disregarding and transgressing upon fundamental principles, rationalizing their philosophy with their social and economic system, and applying it in the determination of governmental policies through control of political parties, they had forestalled policies which might, even in a remote degree, weaken slavery, had limited policies to whatever did not conflict with the peculiar interests of the South, and had promoted policies which were to the advantage of slaveholders at the expense of other sections.

(4) The greatest of all offenses had been with respect to the territories, new slave states, and the domestic slave trade. Having gone as far as possible toward ending the system, the Convention conferred upon Congress the necessary powers to complete their work: control over the foreign slave trade, interstate commerce, the territories, and the admission of states. Article I, Section 9, of the Constitution read: "The migration or importation of such persons as any of the States now existing shall think proper to admit, shall not be prohibited by the Congress prior to the year one thousand eight hundred and eight. . . ." This provision, said the abolitionists was thought at the time to be all that was necessary to enable Congress to destroy slavery, since by it the supply of cheap

[9] *Ibid.*

replacements from Africa could be cut off. It had been used, but the production of a great staple crop, cotton, had so increased the value of slave property as to make slave breeding in this country profitable, had made the upper South instead of Africa the source of supply, and had replaced the African slave trade, which the whole world, including the United States, looked upon with abhorrence and condemned as piracy, by the domestic slave trade, which was even worse. Congress, then, should have used its power over interstate commerce to stop the interstate slave trade.

(5) The power of Congress to exclude slavery from the territories was derived from three sources: the precedent of the Ordinance of 1787; Article IV, Section 3, which said: "The Congress shall have power to dispose of and make all needful rules and regulations respecting the territory or other property belonging to the United States"; and the previously mentioned clause relative to the "migration and importation of persons." No less an authority than John Jay, first Chief Justice of the Supreme Court, held the power of Congress unquestionable under this clause to circumscribe slavery within the limits of the original slave states. The power of Congress to admit or to exclude new states was too obvious to be argued, though there was unlimited opportunity to discuss the conditions which might justify exclusion. Finally, the power of Congress over the District of Columbia was held to be as complete as that of a constitutional convention within a state.

There was remarkable unanimity of opinion among antislavery men on these questions. Beyond that there were all sorts of extreme and questionable interpretations of the powers of Congress over slavery, which led to disagreement even among the uncompromising abolitionists. The more important interpretations were: (1) that slavery had been automatically abolished in all states by the Declaration of Independence, and not having been reëstablished by Congress or the states was illegal everywhere; (2) that slaves had not been deprived of their liberty by due process of law and were entitled to be declared free by the courts; (3) that slavery was an ever-present invitation to foreign invasion, a menace to internal peace and safety, an unending source of discord and internal strife, a detriment to the general welfare, a complete repudiation of the Bill of Rights so far as the Negro was concerned, and that, therefore, Congress had full power, in peace as in war, to abolish it.

Like the Supreme Court, the Southern-rights men did not recognize the Declaration of Independence, or the preamble of the Constitution, as a part of the fundamental law. It is that which gives to the higher-law doctrine of the abolitionists so much historical importance. Lift the organic act of union out of its historical background, concede that the general government created by it is a government of delegated powers, admit an ordinary property right in slaves, and the Constitution becomes, if not a proslavery document, at least a feeble instrument in the hands of slavery's foes. Slavery, said the Southern-rights men, existed previous to the formation of the Constitution and was recognized, not established, by it. Slaves were property, and the definition of property rights was an exercise of sovereign power which was not among the delegations to Congress, but rested with state constitutional conventions, the most sovereign bodies in the entire governmental system. What Congress could not do directly, it could not do by indirection, and any action tending to weaken or to destroy a species of property so intricately bound up with the social and economic life of a section would be a wholly unwarranted assumption of undelegated powers and, therefore, unconstitutional. The primary function of government was protection of persons and property and, since the authority of states could not reach beyond their own limits to perform that important function, it was the duty of the federal government to do so in the territories, on the high

seas, and wherever else its authority extended. The territories were the common property of the states, and every man
had a right to go there with his property and look to the
general government for protection while it remained in the
territorial status. Not until a constitutional convention met
to frame a state constitution preparatory to admission into the
Union could the individual's right of property in slaves or any
other species of property be abrogated, since a territorial
legislature, the creature of Congress, could not exceed the
powers of its creator.

Superior to all questions of the rights, duties, and responsibilities of individual citizens, their state legislatures, and Congress touching upon the institution of slavery was the question
of the powers of the Supreme Court versus those of a state
constitutional convention. The supremacy of the Constitution as a fundamental law was never seriously disputed; or
that there were limitations upon the powers of Congress; or
that the powers of Congress might be enlarged or restricted by
constitutional amendment. Had Congress, immediately after
the Union was formed, excluded slavery from the territories,
prohibited the internal slave trade, and refused to admit any
more slave states, as abolitionists claimed should have been
done, the distinctive weapon of a constitutional amendment
would have been ready-made to their hands and have greatly
simplified their task. Lamentable as they considered this
dereliction of duty, as evidenced by their constant references
to it, they did not ignore the future possibilities of emancipation by amendment to the federal constitution, but fought
bitterly against the annexation of Texas and for exclusion of
slavery from the territories, and clung tenaciously to the
doctrine of exclusion as a cardinal principle of their platform,
in order that the number of slave states might not be increased.

Their main reliance, however, was upon their ability to
indoctrinate the country and make the antislavery philosophy
the controlling philosophy in the federal government. Con-

gress may have betrayed the founding fathers irrevocably, since slave states already in the Union could not well be thrown out; the Supreme Court may have done likewise in sustaining such legislation as the fugitive slave acts; but Congressional acts could be repealed, new ones enacted, and court decisions reversed.    John Marshall, Daniel Webster, and the Federal School, with their doctrine of federal supremacy and judicial review, had laid the groundwork for the triumph of freedom, if only the antislavery forces could get control of Congress and the presidency and keep control long enough to rejuvenate the Court.   The gentle winds of social philosophy and constitutional interpretation, shifting from the Southwest to the Northwest, would blow through the chambers of the Court and serve the same purpose more rapidly and easily than the amending process provided.

Calhoun's doctrine of concurrent majority was perfectly suited to the defense of Southern rights, but it came too late to do more than lend dignity to the defense of a hopeless cause. Its logic, however, remains impregnable, and its ultimate influence in the realm of political economy unpredictable. Space will not permit a full elaboration of the thesis, but its main points may be stated briefly:

Back of all controversies over governmental policies and constitutional interpretations is some social or economic question of vital concern to a minority of the people.

A minority in the nation at large, in such a controversy, is certain to be a majority in a geographical section and, while helpless to defend itself against action by Congress, is in control of its states.

For that reason the best interests of the greatest number of people can best be served by retaining the broad powers of government in the states and delegating to the central government control over only those matters of general concern.

A written constitution was designed for the protection

of individuals and minorities against the selfish pleasure of majorities.

The federal constitution was an instrument of union between sovereign states which did not agree to unlimited submission to the government created by the compact, but delegated only certain powers to it.

The delegation of powers implied limitations and a power, somewhere, capable of enforcing these limitations, since a government which is the judge of the limits of its own powers would arrogate authority to itself, encroach upon the reserved rights of the states, and become an absolutism.

A majority in the nation at large, if it remained a majority long enough, would control not only Congress and the presidency, but the Supreme Court, and under the doctrine of the federal school, the three departments of the federal government acting harmoniously, there would be no real limitations upon its power, and the rights of minorities and the states would be subject to the will of the majority in a consolidated nation.

Majorities do not search constitutions to discover what the rights of minorities are and, therefore, the only effectual check upon majorities is to place in the hands of minorities, for whose benefit constitutional limitations upon the powers of government have been imposed, the power to enforce the limitations.

Neither the Supreme Court nor Congress, therefore, was properly the judge of the latter's power, but the people of a state meeting in constitutional convention.

A state constitutional convention, the most sovereign body in our governmental system, might interpose its authority to protect its citizens against unconstitutional acts of the federal government and determine the mode and measure of redress, even to the point of severing the bonds of union.

Very little was said about the constitutional right of secession during the early years of the controversy, although there

was much discussion of its probability.    A few radical abolitionists favored secession, and some were for throwing the
slave states out; but for the most part the abolitionists were
engaged in counteracting the repeated threats of the South to
secede by belittling the probability of such an occurrence.
Considering the early date, Birney's reply to Elmore in 1838
contains a remarkable exposition of why abolitionists did not
fear secession of the South: secession would increase rather
than decrease discussion of the slavery question about which
the South complained so bitterly; it would introduce discussion into the South itself, invite incitations to insurrection,
increase the number of fugitives, and prevent their recovery,
drive non-slaveholding whites out, and hasten emancipation.
Finally, there was the insurmountable difficulty of accomplishing separation because of the disintegrating forces which
would be unloosed within the South and because of the bonds
of union which could not be dissolved.

Birney's statement concerning the invisible bonds of union
constituted the real, though indirect, reply to the compact
theory.    The historian is impressed by the similarity between
Birney's argument in 1838 and the editorials of those Southern
newspapers which were opposed to secession in 1860.    Said
Birney: "The separation, at the worst, can only be *political*.
There will be no chasm—no rent made in the earth between
the two sections.    The natural and ideal boundaries will
remain unaltered.    Mason and Dixon's line will not become
a wall of adamant that can neither be undermined nor sur-
mounted.    The Ohio river will not be converted into flame,
or into another Styx, denying a passage to every living thing
. . . the multiform interests of the two sections would, in the
main, continue as they are.    The complicated ties of commerce could not be suddenly unloosed. . . .    The newspapers
of the North . . . would be more sought after by the readers of
the South than they now are; and the southern journals would
become doubly interesting to us.    There would be the same

lust for our northern summers and your southern winters . . .
the same desire of marrying and being given in marriage that
now exists between the North and South.    Really it is difficult
to say *where* this long threatened separation is to *begin;* and
if the place of beginning could be found, it would seem like a
poor exchange for the South, to give up all these pleasant and
profitable relations and connections for the privilege of enslaving an equal number of their fellow-creatures."[10]

[10] *Correspondence, between the Hon. F. H. Elmore, One of the
South Carolina Delegation in Congress, and James G. Birney, One of
the Secretaries of the American Anti-Slavery Society* (Anti-Slavery Ex-
aminer, No. 8; New York, 1838), pp. 40–41.    Hereafter cited as *Birney–
Elmore Correspondence.*

# VI. THE LIBERTY PARTY

THE organized movement for the entire abolition of slavery in the United States, culminating with the adoption of the Thirteenth Amendment in 1867, functioned through four successive organizations: the American Anti-Slavery Society, the Liberty Party, the Free Soil Party, and the Republican Party. The movement itself was continuous, aggressive, and progressive, and neither its platform of principles nor its ultimate objective ever changed. The means by which it proceeded to carry its views into effect underwent profound alteration in 1839–40.

Abolitionists recognized from the first, and so stated in the constitution of the American Anti-Slavery Society, that, in all probability, slavery could be entirely abolished only by action of the several slave states. By state law it was sustained, and by state constitutional amendment alone could it be destroyed. Abolition by amendment of the Federal Constitution they regarded as impossible of attainment unless such states as Virginia and Kentucky should become free. Evidence is very convincing, however, that their original objective, even with respect to the slave states, was to abolish slavery and to elevate the Negro by a program of education and persuasion, each state acting for itself; and it is reasonable to assume they would have been successful at an early date had the right of free inquiry not been interdicted in the South and that section almost hermetically sealed against abolitionists and abolition arguments. One is forced to the melancholy reflection that this was the first irrevocable step toward a trial of armed strength—irrevocable because, in a movement such as this, there is no retracing of steps. Free discussion in the South, under all circumstances, might have led to gradual

emancipation through a transition stage of peonage or modified feudalism, without the subject becoming a political question and men's passions being inflamed by the fierce fires of
the hustings.   It certainly would have prevented the political
contest, had it come to that, from becoming sectional in character.

Abolitionists aimed also, from the first, at influencing Congress to prohibit the internal slave trade, abolish slavery in the
territories and the District of Columbia, and prevent its extension to new states.   To these aims may be added the revolutionary objective of the higher-law doctrine, which would ob-
ligate all government functionaries to make decisions, when
possible, in harmony with the principles of the Declaration of
Independence, rather than by the strict letter of the Constitution.   This was the clear statement of the objectives and
intentions of the founders of the American Anti-Slavery
Society, and those of the Republican Party in 1860, so far as
slavery was concerned, were pretty clearly the same.

Organizations and men grow old—their interests and view-
points change.   The antislavery movement, under the direction of the Executive Committee of the American Anti-Slavery
Society and its secretaries—of Theodore Weld, Lewis Tappan,
James G. Birney, Elizur Wright, Joshua Leavitt, and John G.
Whittier—had been aggressive and progressive, had attained
maturity and dignity.   Few movements of this sort ever re-
cede, and this one had been propelled by the ineptitude of its
opponents.   Hostility in the North to a free discussion of the
slavery question and, in some measure, belief in the inherent
degradation of the Negro, were breaking down.   Terms of
scorn and derision were no longer hurled indiscriminately at
abolitionists; too many men of prominence and standing in
their communities were among their number.   A conservative estimate classed one in twenty of the adult population as
an abolitionist, with many times that number staunch sup-
porters of the civil rights of abolitionists, though unwilling to

espouse their cause. In one year (1837–38), the national society alone published 7,877 bound volumes, 47,250 tracts and pamphlets, 4,100 circulars, and 10,490 prints. Its *Quarterly Anti-Slavery Magazine* had an annual circulation of 9,000 copies; *The Slave's Friend,* for children, 131,050; the monthly *Human Rights,* 189,400; and the weekly *Emancipator,* 217,000. Aside from these, there were an estimated one hundred antislavery newspapers throughout the free states, innumerable depositories for the sale of publications, and an increasingly friendly daily press. A large staff of antislavery lecturers was supported in the field by the national and state organizations. Yet the conviction grew daily among far-seeing men that complete triumph of freedom was long distant.

Unable to penetrate the South directly, the abolitionists had hoped to bore in through the great national institutions: the Presbyterian, Methodist, and Baptist churches and the Whig and Democratic parties. Their experience was no more satisfying than it had been with colonization. They got exactly nowhere against the dead weight of inertia, the power of precedent and tradition, and the influence of bread-and-butter expediency upon the membership of institutions. Although the separation of the Baptist and Methodist churches did not come until 1845 and 1846, of the Whig Party until 1852, and of the Democratic Party until 1860, it was perfectly clear by 1839 that, if the effort should be persisted in, separation would result and abolition be no further toward attainment of its objective: complete emancipation by action of the South itself.

The proscription of Thomas Morris by the Democrats and the attempted proscription of Joshua Giddings by the Whigs were unmistakable signs of how far the parties were prepared to go to purge themselves of abolition influence. Morris, senator from Ohio, had ventured to speak in opposition to Calhoun's resolutions of 1837, and in consequence the Democratic Ohio State Legislature had refused to reëlect him to the United States Senate.  He then engaged with Henry Clay in the first great debate on slavery in the Senate and was read completely out of his party.  Giddings was more fortunate in that he was a member of the House of Representatives from a Congressional district which included the Western Reserve of Ohio—a district which, incidentally, had been thoroughly abolitionized by the Lane Seminary boys.  When the Whig caucus in Congress censured him for his antislavery efforts he resigned, stood for reëlection, and was returned to the House by a large majority vote.  As a result of this demand for party regularity on the slavery question Birney and others arrived at the conviction that no *national* organization ever could embrace abolition doctrine, because no man could be a member of such an organization and continue to reside in the South; and that, so long as abolitionists remained in the Whig and Democratic parties, they would find themselves in the unenviable position of having to cast their ballots for slaveholders or for Northern men whose principles were wholly satisfactory to the South.

It is essential to remember that two extremist groups had developed within the American Anti-Slavery Society.  Alvan Stewart had led a movement to amend its constitution and commit the society to an endorsement of the idea that the Constitution of the United States was an antislavery document and direct action by Congress for its abolition in all the states a constitutional procedure.  William Lloyd Garrison had gone to the other extreme of denouncing the Constitution of the United States as a proslavery document, endorsing all sort of vagaries, chief of which were no-human-government and woman's rights, and trying to force *them* upon the society —and had succeeded only in making the antislavery movement ridiculous in the sight of many conservative people.  The louder the Garrisonian group proclaimed their thesis of Christian anarchy, the more imperative direct political action appeared to be to the conservatives in order to save the cause.

The American Anti-Slavery Society, meanwhile, was falling of its own weight. The financial panic which gripped the country after 1837 increased the difficulty of securing funds, and the enormous growth of state societies to the point of maintaining their own presses and corps of lecturers led to duplication of efforts, friction over priority rights, and conflicts of authority. Arthur and Lewis Tappan, the wealthy patrons of numerous benevolent enterprises, were encountering financial difficulties. Theodore Weld's voice was gone, his health was precarious, and his family and farm were demanding more and more of his energies. James G. Birney, two private fortunes exhausted by his interest in abolition, five sons ready for college, and a strong physique nearing the breaking point, had determined to retire to private life and reënter the practice of law. Henry B. Stanton, engaged to marry, felt obliged to fit himself to earn some money. All the old antislavery agents throughout the country were now occupied in some sort of remunerative work, with abolition as an avocation, or were about to be forced to it by the collapse of the whole agency system of the parent society. These men had carried the burden when abolition was a strange, new doctrine and when to advocate it was to incur social and political ostracism. They were the pioneers. Abolition was now a respectable subject for discussion in polite circles. New leadership, new methods, and new types of organization were inevitable.

When Garrison gained control of the American Anti-Slavery Society in 1840, it had outlived its usefulness and was little but a name. Those who were most disturbed by his injection of woman's rights into the movement reorganized as the American and Foreign Anti-Slavery Society, but neither organization was of much importance, except for a few men whose personal influence was derived from their long records of service in the cause. In a practical sense, the old national symbol of antislavery effort ceased to exist, and another was reared in its place—an independent political party. Concerted effort for moral reform was supplanted by direct political action, yet not entirely so. State societies took over and expanded the work of the old parent society, supporting their official presses, maintaining traveling and local lecturers, publishing pamphlets and tracts of every sort. Pastors continued to preach against slavery, and their parishioners to hold their weekly antislavery prayer meetings. The spirit of Angelina Grimké Weld, Elizabeth Cady Stanton, Lydia Maria Child, Julia Tappan, and Abigail Kelley Foster spread through the land, woman's rights and antislavery discussion were inseparable, and a new generation of children was being reared on antislavery lore. All Christian abolitionists were apostles of freedom, and their influence was felt in the schoolroom, in the home, in the business office, in daily contacts with their fellow men everywhere. Oberlin, Oneida Institute, Illinois College, Knox, all sent forth into the professions young men and women who were thoroughgoing abolitionists.

Men like Theodore Weld and Julius LeMoyne were not convinced that political action was "*essential* as a means to the great end in view." They looked upon it as only another distracting issue such as woman's rights, no-human-government, and peace—collateral questions which would "divide, distract, embarrass and alienate the abolition body, and . . . divert their attention and efforts from the first and grand object." This was particularly true, said LeMoyne, because, "except for the *single object* of our association, no body of men who are associated, are composed of such various and almost incongruous materials—men of all religions and no religion—of all politics and shades of policy—of all habits of thought and prejudices of education and locality—which our country furnishes example."[1]   To this reason for opposition

---

[1] F. Julius LeMoyne to James G. Birney, December 10, 1839, *Birney Letters*, I, 511.

they added the fear of revealing the paucity of their numbers, the impropriety of undertaking to promote a religious enterprise by means of an essentially different character, and the possibility of the movement falling under the control of politicians and vote-getting expediency supplanting principle to the end of an abandonment of high antislavery ground.

Even Henry B. Stanton, favorable to independent political action, counseled delay until after the election of 1840. "The Whig Abolitionists," said he, "will go for Harrison despite conscience, consistency, denunciation, and rebuke. . . . There is a perfect mania on the subject of politics, and especially among the Whigs, and you know 49/50ths of our friends are in that party. . . . They would wade to their armpits in molten lava to drive Van Buren from power. . . . Our strongest abolition friends *swear* they will take the liberty to make one more effort to displace Van Buren, and whatever is the result they will then go with us. *They speak truly.* The next election will exorcise the evil spirit which possesses them. Why war with the inevitable?"[2]

This new band of crusaders, however, like the Lane Seminary rebels, were not to be deterred from the task to which they had put their hands. On October 23 of that year they were unsuccessful in their attempt to commit a national assembly of antislavery men at Cleveland to independent nominations; but three weeks later, at Warsaw, New York, a convention of five hundred delegates did adopt the policy and nominated James G. Birney and Julius LeMoyne for president and vice president. The meeting, however, was regarded as too local in character to justify final action. On January 20, 1840, Gerrit Smith, Myron Holley, and William L. Chaplin met at Rochester, New York, went to Arcade, and there succeeded in persuading the New York state convention to call a national antislavery convention for April 1. The convention was

[2] Henry B. Stanton to James G. Birney, March 21, 1840, *ibid.,* pp. 542-543.

held at Albany, and, LeMoyne having declined the nomination, Thomas Earle of Pennsylvania was named on the ticket with Birney. In a letter to the *Friend of Man*, February 8, 1840, Gerrit Smith spoke of it as the "Liberty Party," and so it came to be known.

Most antislavery men, among the rank and file, were opposed to independent political action in the beginning, largely, of course, because they were good Whigs or good Democrats. Political creeds were an inheritance and a habit, soul-deadening and death-defying. However much men might deprecate the proslavery bent of their party leaders and party platforms, or be willing to annoy them with embarrassing questions relative to slavery, they were not willing to take any action which might lead to the dissolution of their party or to withhold a vote which might enable the opposition to win. Slavery was an important issue, one capable of sorely disturbing the conscience and freighted with dire consequences to the national security, but so were other things—banking, for instance, or the tariff, or internal improvement, or the disposition of the public lands—and men were not willing to forego registering a vote on such questions, even though they appreciated the importance of a powerful protest vote against slavery domination of the old line parties.

To all such staunch party men Birney wrote: "The security of life—of liberty—of civil and religious privileges—of the rights of conscience—of the right to use our own faculties for the promotion of our own happiness—of free locomotion,—all these, together with the defence of the barriers and outposts thrown around them by the laws, constitute the highest concerns of the government. These, for the last six years, we have seen invaded one after another—the administration aiding in the onset—till the *feeling of security* for any of them has well nigh expired. A censorship of the mail is usurped by the deputy postmasters throughout more than half of the country, and approved by the administration under which it takes place. The pillage of the Post Office is perpetrated in one of our principal cities, and its contents made a bonfire of in the public square;—no one is brought in question for the outrage. Free speech and debate on the most important subject that now agitates the country, is rendered impossible in our national legislature; the *right* of the people to petition Congress for a redress of grievances is formally abolished by their own servants! And shall we sit down and dispute about the currency, about a subtreasury or no-sub-treasury, a bank or no-bank, while such outrages on constitutional and essential *rights* are enacting before our eyes?"[3]

Many of those who first supported independent political action were convinced of its efficacy as a method of rendering slavery odious and of forcing one or the other of the old parties to adopt a firmer stand against slavery. So far as Myron Holley, James G. Birney, Alvan Stewart, Joshua Leavitt, William Goodell, and others were concerned, however, it represented a settled conviction that the attempt to maintain a harmonious union between sections with such diametrically opposite principles was impossible, and that the time had come for those who believed in the republican principles and habits of the Northern states to make a militant stroke for control of the federal government and thereby gain complete ascendency over the slave power. It was the first step in the formation of two great sectional parties which were to contend for control of the government in 1860, and men knew it to be so. Said Weld: "Nothing short of miracles, constant miracles, and such as the world has never seen can keep at bay the two great antagonist forces. . . . They must drive against each other, till *one* of them goes to the bottom. *Events,* the master of men, have for years been silently but

[3] James G. Birney to Myron Holley, Joshua Leavitt, and Elizur Wright, Jr., May 11, 1840, *ibid.*, pp. 566–567.

without a moment's pause, settling the basis of two great parties, the nucleus of one slavery, of the other freedom."[4]

Why Weld did not favor independent political action is difficult to determine, because he would not discuss it. He labored diligently in Washington during two sessions of Congress, carrying almost the entire burden of outlining the strategy and arguments for the defense of Adams and Giddings against the party purge. He spent every waking hour of the day, in conjunction with Joshua Leavitt, encouraging and inspiring the little group of antislavery Whigs in Washington —Giddings, Adams, Slade, Gates—to more militant action against the slave power, knowing that every blow shook the Whig party to its foundations. There is some evidence that he believed the objectives of the abolitionists would be reached only through the flames of insurrection and civil war. Yet he would not support the Liberty Party, probably because he realized the degree to which political action closed the pulpits of the churches to continued support of the movement. A pastor might with propriety encourage his parishioners to attend a Wednesday night prayer meeting for the slave, but could hardly lend his open support to such a meeting if he knew it would amount to a caucus of the local membership of a political party.

The organization of the Liberty Party marked the beginning of two decades of party chaos. Never before had a party been launched with less sacrifice of principle to vote-getting expediency. It was a party without politicians and without a platform in the ordinary meaning of the word. It embraced but one idea: hostility to slavery. Birney's character and reputation, his inflexible hostility to slavery in all its aspects, and his Christian piety were the party's platform. For six years he strove valiantly to keep the party intact and the movement from patronizing expediency at the expense of

[4] Theodore D. Weld to James G. Birney, January 22, 1842, *ibid.*, II, 663.

principle, as he thought. It was inevitable that, as old party ties weakened, a union of all antislavery men in the North should take place, and the only question was with respect to the conditions of union.

The Whig Party bore the brunt of the third-party onset. Abolitionism represented a religious and intellectual impulse, and wealth, culture, and intelligence were in the Whig Party. Merchants, divines, educators, lawyers, doctors, and the great landed gentry of western New York, Pennsylvania, and Ohio were Whigs. Moreover, the Whig Party never was a national party. It was a political coalition, and only because it refused to undertake a definition of slavery issues did it continue to put presidential candidates into the field long after the southern section of the party was Southern rights in its philosophy and the northern section antislavery in its philosophy. Both old parties were under a continuously increasing strain during these two decades. Men had to satisfy their constituents in the North of their soundness on the slavery question, then meet with their Southern colleagues, draw up platforms and nominate candidates which could be defended on the hustings. The Whigs solved the problem by not touching the question in their national platform and by leaving each state organization free to do as it pleased. The Democrats solved it by framing their national platform in ambiguous language which could be interpreted one way in the North and another in the South. The Whig technique allowed a more rapid infiltration of antislavery doctrine in the North and increased the danger of early separation.

The great question of the terms on which antislavery men would unite for political action was clarified by the campaign of 1844. Birney was deluged with questions about his views on the tariff, a national bank, the disposition of the public lands, Sabbath observance, the Masonic Lodge, and the principles of democratic government. It was perfectly clear, after the election, that the antislavery party of the future must define its position on all the great questions that called for legislative action.   It was equally clear that the extreme view of slavery as being unconstitutional and therefore subject to direct abolition by Congressional action must be sloughed off the creed.   Whig Party leaders, in a desperate effort to stave off defeat, had resorted to outright forgery to discredit Birney, create the impression there was a working agreement between Liberty men and Democrats, and hold the anti-Texas-Annexation vote for Clay.   They failed, since Birney received enough votes in New York to elect Polk, and, as it turned out, annex Texas, involve the country in war with Mexico, and add a vast new territory to the national domain.

The bitterness arising from this episode, together with Birney's devasting articles against Clay's record, insured that staunch Whigs would never enlist under the Liberty Party banner.

The defeat of Van Buren for the nomination of the Democratic Party because of his opposition to annexation drove him out of the party and carried with him many Democrats of antislavery leanings.   Clay's attempt to straddle the question of annexation swept a host of proslavery Whigs out of the party in the South and into the Democratic Party.   The Whig Party never recovered from the blow, Taylor and Fillmore's election in 1848 being possible only through adroit evasion of the slavery question in the national convention and extreme endorsement of Southern rights in the South and flirtation with abolitionism in the North.   Birney's poll of 67,000 votes in 1844, representing a bare fraction of the potential antislavery vote in the country, left no further possibility for evasion of slavery as an issue to be dealt with by politicians.

Soon after the election of 1844 evidences appeared on every hand of how eager antislavery men were to turn from the one idea.   The Ohio and Michigan groups took the lead: Gamaliel Bailey and Salmon P. Chase through the columns of the *Philanthropist* at Cincinnati, and Theodore Foster and

Guy Beckley with the *Signal of Liberty* at Ann Arbor. On December 7, 1845, Foster wrote to Birney: "I am more and more convinced by reflection that the antislavery feeling alone will never bring over to the Liberty Party a majority of all the voters of the United States. We must have some other motives to present to people, which will appeal directly to their own interests. Unless we secure support from other considerations we shall never, as a party, become a majority, and our *principles* will find some other channel of operation than the Liberty Party."[5] Foster and Beckley published a circular to all the antislavery newspapers, explaining their views about what the new party platform ought to be, but received little favorable response. In March, 1847, therefore, Beckley published his program of coöperation with all men who were willing to act upon the following principles:

(1) Equal political rights to all men.

(2) Personal liberty laws similar to those of New Hampshire, Vermont, and Massachusetts.

(3) Repeal of the fugitive slave laws and abolition of slavery in the District of Columbia.

(4) Non-extension of slavery to new states or territories.

(5) Non-support of any man for office who was a slaveholder or would elevate or appoint a slaveholder to office.

Beckley's proposed program envisioned a combination of pressure party politics and independent political action, designed to force all existing parties or parties-to-be to acceptance of the antislavery creed. Events rapidly gave prominence to this platform of principles, to which nothing had been added and little taken away since the organization of the Anti-Slavery Society in 1833, as the ideal platform for an appeal to the electorate. Polk's expansion policy and a rush of settlers to the new domain brought principles, politicians,

[5] Theodore Foster to James G. Birney, December 7, 1845, *ibid.*, p. 982.

and governmental policies to a crisis from which there was no escape and suddenly gave new importance to the oldest and, among abolitionists, the most widely accepted principle of the antislavery creed: the power and duty of Congress to exclude slavery from the territories and to refuse admission to any more slave states.

Shortly after Beckley published his proposed party platform, David Wilmot of Pennsylvania introduced in Congress his famous resolution providing for the exclusion of slavery from any territory which might be acquired from Mexico. William L. Yancey of Alabama promptly clarified the Southern-rights position on that important question by forcing through the legislature of his state the equally famous Alabama Platform emphasizing the power and duty of Congress to protect persons of any and all states in the enjoyment of any and all kinds of property in the territories so long as they remained in the territorial status.

Thenceforth nothing new was added in the way of principles on either side of the controversy. Two opposing and utterly incompatible political philosophies were in the ascendancy, one in the South, the other in the North. They were Calhoun's doctrine of concurrent majority and Birney's doctrine of the higher law. Inextricably woven into these constitutional theories was the question of slavery. Two national political parties were in existence, serving as the cement of the nation. The great question was how long these two parties could survive the trend toward political sectionalism both North and South. Every aspect of the slavery question was a potential threat to their existence: the interstate slave trade, slavery in the District of Columbia, the fugitive-slave and personal-liberty laws, admission of states, and the organization of territories. No one of these problems could be considered and solved on its own merits. Each was a symbol for the whole, and the contest was waged over the territorial question simply because the acquisition of a vast new domain and the rush of settlers to it required the organization of territorial governments.

The attempt to pull all antislavery men out of the Whig and Democratic parties and into a Northern sectional party had been in progress ten years. The one idea of hostility to slavery had failed to accomplish it, and both the Liberty Party name and the principle of a one-idea platform were abandoned. Congressional exclusion of slavery from the territories was now emphasized and, eventually, that which Foster and Beckley had held to be so essential—a principle of direct appeal to the personal interests of the voter—was discovered: free homesteads to settlers. We shall see how perfectly it filled this need and likewise met the tests of an antislavery measure.

# VII. THE SPIRIT OF THE MISSISSIPPI VALLEY: NORTHWEST VERSUS SOUTHWEST[1]

THE Old Southwest was the stronghold of slavery; it ruled the country during the thirty years' war over that institution and it led the exodus from the Union in the end. The Old Northwest began the organized crusade against slavery, carried it through to a successful conclusion, and saved the Union in the process. Here in the Mississippi Valley was a turmoil of interests, impulses, and ideals from which emerged great intellects and great personalities, fighting for supremacy in the minds and hearts of men. I thoroughly believe that, had the region east of the mountains somehow been blotted out in 1830 and these two western regions been an entity unto themselves, things would not have happened very much differently from what they did, though they would have occurred much more quickly.

John C. Calhoun of South Carolina developed the compact theory of the Constitution and the doctrine of concurrent majority into an intelligible thesis for the defense of the South within the Union. Barnwell Rhett of that state, through the columns of the *Charleston Mercury,* first sounded the tocsin of disunion; but it was men like William L. Yancey of Alabama, Jefferson Davis of Mississippi, Pierre Soulé and Judah P. Benjamin of Louisiana, who combined the two into a practical program for secession, preached it and popularized

---

[1] For want of other simple terms by which to designate the regions west of the Alleghenies I am taking the liberty of using the terms "Mississippi Valley," "Old Southwest," and "Old Northwest" in a much broader sense than is customary among historians, and am including not only Georgia and Alabama, but western New York, western Pennsylvania, and the region of the Great Lakes.

it until men came to regard it as a legitimate and secure final refuge for their institutions. Without Yancey's brilliant oratory and indefatigable labors there would have been no secession, no Southern Confederacy. It was he who wrote the Alabama Platform, that comprehensive statement of the right of slaveholders to enter the territories and be protected by the federal government. It was he who committed Alabama, one year before the election, to a secession convention in the event of a Republican victory, forced the issue of Southern rights to a conclusion in the Charleston Convention, and wrote the platform of the Constitutional Democracy. It was Stephen A. Douglas of Illinois who developed the doctrine of popular sovereignty, as destructive to slavery in the territories as Congressional exclusion; and it was Senator George E. Pugh of Ohio, who, as spokesman for the Democrats of the Northwest, told the Charleston Convention they could not endorse the Alabama Platform without personal dishonor and the disruption of their party at home and that they would not do so.

It was Theodore Weld and his little group of antislavery apostles who first denounced slavery as a sin and abolitionized Ohio. It was Joshua Giddings of Ohio, one of Weld's first converts, who defied the Whig Party in its attempt to muzzle his attacks upon slavery in Congress, and it was the voters of the Western Reserve who sent him back in triumph when he resigned and stood for reëlection. It was Thomas Corwin of Ohio who said in Congress he hoped the Mexicans would welcome our soldiers with bloody hands to hospitable graves; it was Corwin who was chairman of the Committe of Thirty-three, chosen to effect conciliation in 1860–61; it was the Ohio delegation that cast ten of the twenty-eight votes against forming the Committee; and that committee was turned into a graveyard for every compromise presented in the House. It was Birney, then a backwoods farmer of an Indian settlement on the frontier of Michigan, who clarified and popularized the higher-law doctrine, and was the first candidate of

the antislavery forces for the presidency. It was the abolitionists of western New York who organized the Liberty Party,
and it was the same original group of Birney abolitionists in
Michigan who organized the Republican Party at Jackson,
Michigan, fourteen years later.

Benjamin Lundy began his *Genius of Universal Emancipation* at Mount Pleasant, Ohio, moved it to Tennessee, then
to Baltimore, and finally to Illinois, where he trained Zebina
Eastman to carry on after his death. Eastman moved it to
Chicago, called it the *Western Citizen,* and published it
through the aid of a wealthy patron of Abraham Lincoln, who
only asked, in return for financial assistance, that a copy of
every issue be sent to Lincoln. It was Lincoln who worsted
Douglas in the great preliminary skirmish of the campaign of
1860; who delivered his "House Divided" speech six months
in advance of Seward's "Irrepressible Conflict" speech; who
carried every state in the Old Northwest, and New York and
Pennsylvania by a clear majority of the popular votes; who
refused to compromise on the only basis even remotely acceptable to the South; and who never gave the slightest intimation
that he ever entertained for a moment the thought of recog-
nizing the legality of secession. It is my opinion that the old
ideas about Lincoln not being an abolitionist and his elevation
to power not being a menace to the institution of slavery are
wholly wrong. The South was absolutely correct in its estimate of what had happened in the presidential election of
1860, even though it may have been wrong in its decision as
to the proper course of action. By 1860 Lincoln was the
living embodiment of antislavery doctrine and antislavery
action. Let us look a little more deeply into the impulses of
this section.

As the original states east of the mountains grew in stature
after the Revolution, the prescriptive rules of precedence and
conformity, the adversity which dogs the steps of all but the
favored few, and the sanguine expectation of better things

beyond the horizon drove men far outside the limits of established government. Whether they came together elsewhere by slow convergence or moved en masse, the time inevitably arrived when recognition of land claims, suppression of crime, common defense, and inheritance required that orderly processes of government must prevail. It was then that, pooling knowledge and ideas, men launched new commonwealths. Initial stages were often crude, and simple as the need required; but, ultimately, states emerged, and the process constitutes an epitome of self-government. What was begun through necessity eventually came to be regarded as an inherent right and squatter sovereignty an unwritten precept of public policy. Stephen A. Douglas, master of ambiguity and politician par excellence, finding the northern wing of the Democracy trapped between the proslavery protectionists of the Black Belt and the rising tide of antislavery exclusionists in the Old Northwest, seized upon it as a drowning man seizes a life belt, and staked his political fortunes upon the right of the first settlers in a territory to decide the question of slavery for themselves. Illogical as it was, popular sovereignty gave him 1,365,000 votes in 1860, so deep-rooted was the idea of self-determination in the philosophy of the people. The ease with which the poor man could push on to the frontier with his rifle and his axe, as compared with the encumbrances of the migrating slaveholder, made popular sovereignty a practical application of abolition objectives, and equal anathema to the South. Douglas had an abolition technique without an abolition philosophy.

Here, also, was the arena of land speculation during the period. Land, with its food-producing soil, its timber resources, its mineral deposits, its water power, and its countless sites for cities drew teeming millions toward the setting sun. Whether their dreams centered about a little plot whereon to build a home or about the unearned increment to be derived from speculations, land meant freedom, security, per-

chance wealth. From Byrd and Washington to Slidell and
Douglas private fortunes were built from land speculation;
and the record of those in public life who turned aside to
gamble reads like a Who's Who of revered statesmen. So
great was the wealth to be derived from bringing land and
slaves together in the Old Southwest that men deliberately
abandoned plantations in the older sections, the price of
slaves trebled in twenty years, traffic in human flesh became a
commercial enterprise, and the yeomanry retreated into the
upcountry or hurried on to new frontiers. The Old Northwest, lacking slaves and staple crops, remained a land of
sturdy yeomen, diversified agriculture, and self-sufficing communities. The distressed of many lands poured in to claim
their quota of nature's stores and swell the chorus of liberty,
fraternity, and equality for all men. Men wanted land, and
what His Majesty, King James, began with the touch of the
regal pen, those who held the portfolio of land administration
thereafter never ceased. The states reluctantly surrendered
western lands to the federal government because public lands
constituted a great treasure which gave power to those who
controlled them. The government rewarded the veterans of
its early wars with lands, and sold to all on easy terms, but the
Republican Party, the party of youth and daring and vision,
would have been twice foolish had it missed so rare an opportunity to capture farmers' votes. Twice foolish because the
Democratic Party was the party of agrarianism, with its intellectual leadership in the Black Belt and voting power in
the rich prairies of Ohio and Illinois; and because the
Southern slaveholders had long opposed the priority rights of
settlers. And so the Republican promise of a free homestead
of 160 acres to every settler was a more powerful thrust at
slavery than their threat of Congressional exclusion. It dis-
rupted the Democratic Party and pledged new states to
freedom.

Europe had promised little but a potter's field for many

who were to find America equally unmerciful. Death claimed thousands during the period of acclimatization. It was ever thus. As waves of emigrants rolled westward, pestilence, privation, and toil decimated their ranks until the continent became one vast sepulcher, and for every child who grew to manhood it seemed another died. The paths of inland travel were strewn with unmarked graves, and little mounds on every homestead site bore tragic witness to the cost of empire. Early marriages, large families, and stern Calvinistic faith attest the powers of adaptation in the race. Listen to the noble Birney's letter of condolence to Gerrit Smith: "In the spring of '33, during my absence from home in the South, a charming boy between five and six, and, *then,* our only daughter between three and four years old were taken away by the *Scarlet* fever within three weeks of each other. I had left them, a few weeks before, in fine health. Passing by the Post Office in Natchez, expecting but very little to find a letter for me *there* from home, I inquired, and one was given me informing me of the death of my boy. In New Orleans, in the midst of strangers, almost the very night before I expected to set out for home to sympathize with my anxious family in our loss, a friend stepped up to me in the public room and told me, that my only daughter was dead. Dear, dear bro. I know the riches of God's consolations, for I then felt them, as I trust you, and your dear wife do. What shall we render unto him for all his benefits? It may be, that he has taken your little one from the evil to come, and is preparing you for greater usefulness in the great work to which he is now summoning his children."[2] Men not only made a profession of faith, they lived by faith. Had they not, the strongest among them would have broken under the terrific strain of the uncertainties and sorrows of life. Witness Robert Holman and Birney, the one heading for the heart of the Black Belt, the other

[2] James G. Birney to Gerrit Smith, September 13, 1835, *Birney Letters,* I, 242–243.

pressing north to the land of freedom, kneeling in prayer by the horseback trail in the Kentucky wilderness, seeking guidance for Holman with relation to slavery; or Theodore Weld praying in the office of the hard-fisted attorney, Joshua Giddings, until the latter was convinced of the sin of slavery; or John J. Shipherd plodding along the trails of western Michigan, stopping at sundown to kneel in prayer at the top of a little knoll, rising and pledging his faith that here should be erected an institution of higher learning and Christian brotherhood; or follow Phebe Mathews among the Negroes of Cincinnati, where Weld said: "Often, when exhausted by over-toil, and weak from fasting and insufficient sleep, she threaded obscure lanes and dingy passages, stooping into cellars and climbing to garrets, kneeling on damp floors at dying beds, and weeping with those that wept, in sheds and hovels. She perfectly identified herself with the scorned and persecuted class for whom she was spent. She lived in their families, made them her companions, linked herself to their lot, shared with them their burdens and their bonds, and meekly bowed her head with theirs to the storm that swept over them."[3]  Or listen to the plaintive notes of the imperishable Negro spirituals and judge the importance of that Lane Seminary debate in which the "Sin of Slavery" was first pronounced in solemn tones. Men thought in terms of their children, and the legacy they sought to provide was something different from stocks and bonds and mortgages. They thought in terms of the underprivileged, and it was not in terms of the dole. It was in terms of education, religion, and economic opportunity, those great collateral principles of political democracy: freedom and equality of opportunity for advancement, spiritually, mentally, and economically.

Nowhere else and at no other period of American history did the words "all men are created equal, and endowed by their Creator with the right to life, liberty and the pursuit of

---

[3] "The Late Mrs. P. M. Weed," *Weld–Grimké Letters*, II, 997.

happiness" mean more than in this section during these years. Society was fluid; the acquisitive instinct was unrestrained; every man stood on his own feet and was responsible for his own destiny.   This rugged individualism conquered an inhospitable wilderness, and it figured prominently in emancipation of the slaves.   Alexander H. Stephens came out of the Georgia upcountry with only a yoke of oxen to work his way through school; yet he went into Congress and became vice president of the Confederacy and leading historian of the movement for Southern independence.   Andrew Johnson crossed the mountains as a tailor's apprentice; his wife taught him to read; yet he was elected to the governorship of Tennessee and, finally, succeeded Lincoln to the presidency of the nation.   Jefferson Davis cleared his first plantation largely by the labor of his own hands, became a wealthy planter, United States senator from Mississippi, and president of the Confederate States of America.   Abraham Lincoln, at the age of nine, was taken into the Indiana wilderness with only a linsey-woolsey shirt to cover his nakedness; yet his achievements placed him forever among the world's immortals. Men lived intensely, working hard, dreaming dreams, and achieving great things.   Measure success by the distance a man travels from the circumstances of his birth to the zenith of his career, or by the enduring qualities of his contributions to human happiness and human progress, or by the mundane test of accumulated wealth, and the Valley abounded with successful men.   *Only* in the Northwest the laborer of today prospered and hired his labor tomorrow in never-ending succession; while in the Southwest the laborer today prospered and bought his laborer tomorrow, thereby fixing the latter's status for life and making it increasingly difficult for other men to graduate from the status of poverty.

In the Valley, too, were the expansionists: the war hawks of 1812, including Henry Clay, who wanted Canada; Bickley and his little group who met in a room of a store at Portsmouth, Ohio, and organized the obscure but powerful Knights of the Golden Circle, whose aim was to rear a powerful slave empire with its center at Havana and a radius long enough to include the slave states, Mexico, and Central America; William Walker, the "Grey-Eyed Man of Destiny," and his sponsor, Governor Quitman of Mississippi, who amused themselves with filibustering expeditions to Central America and Cuba; Pierre Soulé, who inspired the Ostend Manifesto; James K. Polk and a host of others, whose expansion policies led to the annexation of Texas and war with Mexico; John C. Frémont, the Pathfinder, unofficial sponsor of the free state of California and first Republican candidate for the presidency; Jefferson Davis, who, as secretary of war, directed the first great surveys for transcontinental railroads; most of them empire builders, the Southerners among them thinking in terms of conquest, of great plantations and rich silver mines; while the millions in the North, no less expansionist in their philosophy, though less grandiose in their dreams, were thinking in terms of homesteads for their sons and daughters and a refuge for the poorest among them.

There are historians who hold that the great mass of people, North and South, were pacifically inclined in 1860 and would have followed the lead of Stephen A. Douglas in adopting a formula of conciliation if they had been permitted to speak in the crisis. That they were not permitted to do so was due, they say, to the machinations of a group of disgruntled politicians from the South who broke up the Union over an abstraction and to Abraham Lincoln, president-elect, who feared that conciliation would disrupt and destroy the Republican Party. There are historians who hold that Lincoln was not an uncompromising foe of the peculiar institutions of the South; that he had never, before assuming the presidency, proposed or pretended to have a solution for the slavery problem; but, instead, admitted his utter inability, if endowed with complete authority in the matter, to offer such a solution; that the circumstances of war and the passions it loosed forced him to face the slavery problem more boldly; that he turned to the stern doctrine of the emancipation proclamation only after unsuccessfully trying compensated emancipation in the border states, and never abandoned hope of effecting some arrangement that might deal more gently and generously with Southern property rights in slaves.

I am constrained to the belief that they are wrong on all these points; that, if Weld and Birney were abolitionists, Lincoln was one; and if they had a plan, he had a better one. Leaving out of consideration every statement reputed to him about which there is the slightest doubt, we still find that he was thoroughly sound on the fundamental principles of abolition doctrine: that the subject of slavery was not a domestic concern of the Southern states, that it was a moral and political evil which menaced the rights of free men, was contrary to the principles enunciated in the Declaration of Independence and a violation of eternal principles of right.

On the question of slavery in its relation to the nonslaveholder we find one significant idea running through all his public pronouncements of the forties and fifties, variously stated according to the exigencies of the occasion, but never retracted: that slavery was hostile to the interests of the poor man, who invariably sought to escape to the free states or to the territories; and that the territories should be kept free by the nation as a haven for the poor. Furthermore, while disclaiming all idea of perfect equality between the races, he did insist over and over, and in unmistakable terms, that the Negro should be free to develop whatever talents he might possess and be protected in his civil right to the enjoyment of the fruits of his own labor. When the Wilmot Proviso was being discussed in Congress, Lincoln was the only Whig member from Illinois, and he voted for it in one form or another not fewer than forty times. He denounced the Dred Scott decision, and said he would not vote for the admission of another slave state.   It is true that, as an aspirant for the Senate seat of Douglas, he said that, much as he hated slavery, he would vote to extend it rather than see the Union dissolved, but two years later, as president-elect, he ordered his party in Congress to "hold fast as with chains of steel" on the territorial question, and refused to endorse a compromise on the basis of restoration of the Missouri Compromise line. His reason for this was not limited to his desire to keep the territories free, but embraced the abolition objective of killing the institution in the slave states by circumscription. Charles Sumner said they purposed to pen it up so it would die like a rat in its hole.   Lincoln said, in 1856: "Let us draw a cordon, so to speak, around the slave states, and the hateful institution, like a reptile poisoning itself, will perish by its own infamy."[4]

What was his attitude toward the fugitive-slave question? In public and as an aspirant for office he avoided the subject as much as possible.   In a private letter to Joshua Speed of Kentucky he wrote: "I confess I hate to see the poor creatures hunted down and caught and carried back to their stripes and unrequited toil; but I bite my lips and keep quiet."[5]   Yet in his inaugural, speaking to the nation for the first time, did he urge obedience to the fugtive-slave law and provisions for its more effective enforcement by the repeal of the personal-liberty laws?   Not at all.   He proposed that the existing fugitive-slave law should be repealed and another be substituted guaranteeing the right of habeas corpus and jury trial to the fugitive, thus advocating what would at one stroke quiet all agitation in the North by effectually providing that no fugitives would ever again be returned.   The abolitionists had tried to do this by state law until the Supreme Court

    [4] "The Lost Speech," *Life and Works of Abraham Lincoln* (Centenary Edition.   9 vols., New York, 1907), II, 300–301.   Hereafter cited as *Works*.
    [5] Abraham Lincoln to Joshua F. Speed, August 24, 1855, *ibid.*, IX, 190.

decision in *Prigg* v. *Pennsylvania* declared Congressional control to be exclusive; and had then turned to personal-liberty laws of doubtful constitutionality. Now that the antislavery forces were coming into control of the federal government, at the first opportunity Lincoln suggested the full use of their new power to settle the question to their complete satisfaction.

Where did Lincoln stand on this question of the nature of the federal government? Did he agree with Calhoun and Southern-rights men that in all cases of dispute between a state and the federal government the state was the judge of the extent of its grievances and of the mode and measure of redress? Did he agree with the Unionists of the slave states that in a similar case the burden of proof was upon the federal government and that the final decision must rest with the amending power in a national convention? Did he agree with the Marshall–Webster school that the Supreme Court was the final arbiter in all disputes between the federal government and the states? With none of them. At Indianapolis, speaking on the subject for the first time only after he had left Springfield for Washington, he startled the nation by saying in effect that the states were political subdivisions of the United States and bore the same relation to the United States that a county bore to a state; and he followed it in his inaugural address by implying that, in all cases of dispute over powers not expressly granted or denied by the Constitution, the minority of the people must submit to the will of the majority, irrespective of Supreme Court decisions. It was a species of consolidation doctrine such as no man in public life had ever before uttered and such as only the most extreme consolidationist could possibly endorse. Put into practical effect it would remove all limits to antislavery legislation.

Finally, there is the question of emancipation. The great leaders among the abolitionists, those who, in the beginning, knew intimately both the North and the South, never had the least expectation that slavery would be peaceably or voluntarily abolished. In 1836 Charles Grandison Finney was pleading with the Lane Seminary boys to become revivalists rather than antislavery agents, with the argument that the unholy excitement raised by abolitionists in church and state would increase and soon end in civil war. Writing to Weld in New York, he was even more emphatic: "Brother Weld is it not true . . . that we are in our present course going fast into civil war? Will not our present movements in abolition result in that? Shall we not ere long be obliged to take refuge in a military despotism? Have you no fear of this? If not, why have you not? Nothing is more manifest to me than that the present movements will result in this, unless your mode of abolitionizing the country be greatly modified. . . . Unless we can come to a better understanding among ourselves, act more harmoniously and wisely and piously, I fear all the evil and horrors of civil war will be the consequence."[6]

Weld did not reply directly to this argument of Finney's; at least, his answer has not been preserved. But he has not left us in doubt as to what he thought and even anticipated with some degree of satisfaction. In a letter to the Grimké sisters in 1838 he said: "The uproar on the Canada border, the Seminoles, Mexicans, the Western and Northwestern Indians, the conflicts in congress, all foreshow a storm blast with God in the midst. I feel in more perfect peace. I rejoice and leap for joy."[7] Four years later, as director and confidential adviser of the antislavery bloc in Congress, he wrote to his wife:

"The almost universal bankruptcy that now whelms the South; the low price of their *only* great staple cotton, and the certainty that the price cannot *rise* on account of the supply

---

[6] Charles Grandison Finney to Theodore D. Weld, July 21, 1836, *Weld–Grimké Letters*, I, 318.

[7] Theodore D. Weld to Sarah and Angelina Grimké, January 5, 1838, *ibid.*, II, 515.

rushing into European markets from immense regions just thrown open to the culture in the east, added to this the necessity of resorting to direct taxation for the support of the national government, the existing difficulties with Great Britain portending war at no great distance; and the certainty that in such a case the first demonstration would be made upon the southern coast and the standard of freedom to the slave unfurled everywhere, all these things and divers others, all brought by God's providence in point blank range, the combustible trains all laid into the very centre of the magazine and the blazing brand waving over them, fills them with rage and consternation.  Oh that they knew in this their day the things that belong to their peace!  The slaveholders of the present generation, if cloven down by God's judgments, cannot plead that they were *unwarned*.  Warnings, reproofs, and the foreshadows of coming retribution have for years freighted the very air, and should sudden destruction come upon them now at last, well may the God of the oppressed cry out against them, 'because I have called and ye have refused. . . .  Therefore will I laugh at your calamity and mock when your fear cometh.' "[8]

Sarah Grimké, devotee of the peace and no-human-government theory, viewed the course of events with apprehension: "Although my faith never swerves about the abolition of slavery, yet at present I have little hope that it will be brought about by peaceful means.  The blood spilt at Alton will be the seed of future discord; those who were engaged in the mob as well as the defenders of the press, will thirst for more, and who can foresee the calamities that await us."[9]

Lincoln expressed the same sentiments in a letter to George Robertson of Kentucky, saying, in effect, that slavery could not be abolished without war: "Since then [1820] experience had demonstrated, I think, that there is no peaceful extinction of slavery in prospect for us. . . . So far as peaceful voluntary emancipation is concerned, the condition of the negro slave in America . . . is now as fixed and hopeless of change for the better, as that of the lost souls of the finally impenitent. The autocrat of all the Russias will resign his crown and proclaim his subjects free republicans sooner than will our American masters voluntarily give up their slaves."[10]

Within one week after his inaugural address, without the knowledge of even his cabinet, he ordered troops into Fort Pickens with the certain knowledge that war would follow, and remarkably soon, considering the tremendous administrative burdens, he proposed compensated emancipation in the District of Columbia and in the border states, but supported by arguments so distinctly foreign to Lincoln's clarity of thought that it is difficult to believe them sincere or made with any hope of endorsement. Lincoln knew, as everyone else did, that the antislavery men had, from the day agitation began, scorned all discussion of compensated emancipation or plans for colonization. These principles were as fundamental and deeply rooted in antislavery doctrine as the sin of slavery itself. Lincoln was one of the shrewdest interpreters of public opinion we have ever had in public life. In his ability to analyze difficult situations he has never been surpassed. As a leader of men he stands alone. In proposing compensated emancipation and colonization he was proposing something he must have known was not acceptable to the Northern people. He was paving the way for—easing the shock of—his Emancipation Proclamation, already formulated in his mind many months before.

From first to last, throughout his entire career, Lincoln was in advance of other public men and of the majority of the people on the slavery issue. On the questions of

[10] Abraham Lincoln to George Robertson, August 15, 1855, *Works,* IX, 56–57.

fugitive slaves, the Dred Scott decision, slavery in the territories, and the exclusion of any more slave states he was thoroughly sound. His Washington Birthday address stamps him as almost a pioneer abolitionist. His "House Divided" speech was delivered six months before Seward's "Irrepressible Conflict" speech and over the protest of his friends. He went to Washington with the Chicago Platform as his gospel and war against the South, the shibboleth of the extremists, as a determined policy. In his Indianapolis speech and his inaugural address, knowing that his every expression would be carefully weighed by millions of men anxious to find in his remarks something to indicate his future policy, he enunciated a political philosophy designed to make the mandates of an unrestrained numerical majority the operative law—it was a complete endorsement of the doctrine of the higher law. And, finally, he did nothing to prevent, if indeed he did not actually precipitate, the war which abolitionists had long hailed as the necessary *modus vivendi* for direct action against slavery.

It is unfortunate that, because he did not hate slaveholders, historians should conclude that he did not hate slavery; and that, because he emphasized the preservation of the Union, emancipation was forced upon him as a means to that end.

The circumstances of Lincoln's early life gave him incomparable human compassion. Few characters are so deeply enshrined in the hearts of so many people; none loved their fellow men more generously than he. For four years he prosecuted the war vigorously, careless of constitutional restraints, but tempering arbitrary action with mercy, and solving as many problems with his heart as with his head, refusing to allow the nation, the heritage of coming generations, to be destroyed by the pride of its enemies or the blunders of its friends, ever mindful of the futility of victory without peace.

We see him, in the last days of the war, standing upon the steps of the Capitol as the armies of Grant and Sherman were closing in a vise the remnant of Lee's gallant army of Virginia. Tall, gaunt, stalwart, with the agony of years finding expression in the deep lines which furrowed his cheeks, but with the inspiration of a great soul suppressing the distress of unbelievable sorrow, speaking his last inaugural:

"Fondly do we hope, fervently do we pray, that this scourge of war may speedily pass away. Yet if God wills that it continue until all the wealth piled by the bondsman's two hundred years of unrequited toil shall be sunk, and until every drop drawn with the lash shall be paid by another drawn with the sword, as was said two thousand years ago, still must it be said that the judgments of the Lord are true and righteous altogether."[11]

Who does not believe he leaned as heavily upon divine providence as the early abolitionists has read those lines to no purpose. His love for the Union was great, but that it was as impelling as his hatred of slavery I cannot believe; and that those who elected him to office were satisfied of his soundness on both points I am firmly convinced.

[11] Richardson, James D., ed., *Messages and Papers of the Presidents* (10 vols., Washington, D.C., 1896–99), VI, 276.

# VIII. THE SECESSION IMPULSE

A PEOPLE who, over a long period of years, practice in-
justice as a part of their daily routine, who feel themselves commissioned by the Creator to develop a superior
type of culture, who become so presumptuous of their lily-
whiteness of character that the slightest aspersion must be
atoned by the blood of the offender, who feel that the product
of their economic system is so essential that desire for it will
outweigh all considerations of humanity and international
faith on the part of others, who claim all the benefits of association and ignore the rules of reciprocity, and who are
so everlastingly sure they are right, that they will not brook
discussion—such a people come eventually to have a distorted
view of everything.  Especially do they feel that those who
oppose them are obnoxious and hate them for being so.

A people who, over a long period of years, bitterly denounce infringement of their own rights as individuals and
minorities by majority opinion in a local community and
then seek to introduce majority rule functioning through the
force of public opinion into the general government, who are
so entranced by the evils of a distant slave economy that they
fail to recognize the evils of their own domestic wage economy, who are so carried away by the hatred of other men's
institutions that they come to hate those men and everyone
who associates with them, who are ready to tear up the finest
instrument of government ever written because it recognizes
an institution prevailing in their own states at the time of
writing, who denounce the courts for according to persons
and property they hate the same protection they claim for
themselves and their own property—such a people, also, are
likely to be obnoxious to those who differ with them.

The extremists in the two sections of the country in 1860 belong in these classifications.    Whether they numbered fifty or fifty thousand is not of much importance.    Sometimes the excesses of one man or a mere handful of men are interpreted as outward manifestation of the character of a whole people, and the generality of people, both North and South, from 1830 to 1860 came more and more to judge the opposing section by the excesses of its extremists.    Republicans were all John Browns to the Southerners, and slaveholders were all Simon Legrees to the Northerners.

No democratic government can survive through a single generation unless there be free and unrestricted inquiry and discussion in the schoolroom, the press, and the public forums. That process makes it possible for people to live happily and harmoniously together, and the more difficult the problems of adjustment, the more essential it is.    Paralyze it and passion, prejudice, and emotionalism prevail.    Destroy the source of an enlightened public opinion and religious fanaticism, class hatreds, or racial antipathies lead straight to inquisition or civil war.    There cannot be said to have been an enlightened public opinion in either section on the questions at issue after Lincoln's election.

In all probability, no man among the Southern leaders could have explained, in a manner completely satisfactory to the historian of today, why the seven states of the lower south seceded from the Union and formed the Confederate States of America in the winter of 1860–61.    A cogent prophecy of what would happen and why it would happen in event a Republican president should be elected was given, however, by *The Kentucky Statesman,* January 6, 1860, almost twelve months before the secession of any state: "The Constitution of the United States, the laws of Congress giving practical force to its guarantees and the decisions of the Supreme Court, expounding and construing the laws, have secured to slave property in the States and Territories all the protection that is claimed and needed."

In short, according to the considered judgment of that paper, the South was perfectly satisfied with the Constitution, with the laws of Congress, and with the decisions of the Supreme Court as they applied to slavery. Nothing which had occurred up to that point would justify a disruption of the Union.

"But there are issues," said the *Statesman*, "and important issues outside the Constitution, which soon must be tried, and these questions will subordinate to their consideration all others not of immediate and practical importance." These issues it listed as:

(1) Repeal of the fugitive-slave law.

(2) Reversal of the Dred Scott decision through reorganization of the Supreme Court.

(3) Abolition of slavery in the territories and exclusion of any more slave states.

(4) Abolition of slavery in the District of Columbia.

(5) Prohibition of the interstate slave trade.

(6) Unceasing war upon the institution in the slave states.

"If the republican party," concluded the *Statesman*, "now a most formidable organization, shall succeed in attaining control of the government, its history leaves no doubt that it will undertake to carry out these purposes, and if so the whole power of the federal executive will not be able to coerce the subjection of seceding states. . . . Its success will overthrow the government and that issue must be tried in 1860."[1]

Exhaustive study of available sources confirms the accuracy of the *Statesman's* perspective and designates Lincoln's election as the pivotal point about which events of 1860–61 turned. Furthermore, we are compelled to recognize the fact that Lincoln's election marked the elevation to power of a party whose philosophy was revolutionary; that a twofold revolution was in progress in the United States after

[1] *The Kentucky Statesman*, January 6, 1860, in Dumond, Dwight L., ed., *Southern Editorials on Secession* (New York, 1931), pp. 3–5.

1830; and that Lincoln's election marked the conclusion of one phase of it and the organization of the Confederate States of America the culmination of the other phase. It is essential here to recount briefly the nature and progress of this twofold revolution.

The Fathers of the Constitution wove a rich Anglo-Saxon heritage of human rights into the fabric of the Union. They added to this, however, three unique and distinctly American contributions to the science of government: (1) they provided for the protection, by written constitutions, of minorities and of individuals against the unrestrained will of majorities; (2) they wrote into the federal constitution the cardinal principles of Jeffersonian democracy, that government is good in proportion as it is kept close to the people, and that the general government should be a government of limited, delegated powers, all others residing in the states or the people; (3) they made provision for the admission of new states to the Union on a basis of perfect equality with the original thirteen, with no restriction upon the nature of their institutions other than that they must have republican forms of government. Subsequently, in adding new states to the Union, state lines were drawn here, there, and everywhere, so that in the end there was scarcely a state that did not have within its limits cities and diversified industries, agriculture and commerce, a medley of racial stocks, religious sects and social customs; and there was not a natural geographical section of the nation but was divided among many states.

Every year that has passed in the century and a half of the Republic's life has multiplied evidences of the importance of these structural elements.

Retention of broad powers of government in the states —powers that are derived from the people of a state and not from the whole people through the medium of the general government—has allowed for the greatest possible differences in legislation intimately touching the lives of the people, and for the greatest possible experimentation in social legislation without friction, since minorities are reduced to a minimum. It gave to the nation as many experimental laboratories as there were states—an asset the value of which was greatly enhanced by the westward movement, with its continuous process of state making. Division of natural geographical regions among many states gave to each state the natural basis for a two-party system of government, encouraged sufficient similarity of development and homogeneity to permit the two-party system to be national in scope, and provided the least possible encouragement to those prejudices and jealousies arising out of geographical sectionalism which have ever been found to be a source of disquietude to the public mind and pregnant with mischievous consequences to the country.

The Constitution forbade certain powers to Congress, certain powers to the state governments, certain powers to both governments. These limitations upon Congress and state legislatures are for the protection of minorities against the tyranny of majorities. Majorities can be just as despotic as any emperor has ever been. In our nation a minority on any social and economic question may always hold up between themselves and the advancing might of the majority, who make the laws, the Constitution and say: "Thus far shalt thou come and no farther." Back of every alignment of men into political parties, of every dispute over legislation and constitutional interpretation, are social or economic questions which vitally touch the lives and fortunes of the people. A minority on any question today is likely to be a majority in one or more states, and to be a majority in the nation at large tomorrow. While still a minority in the nation at large it may inaugurate its proposed reform in one or more states. It may never get beyond that; but, if it becomes a majority in the nation, it may be unable to translate its ideas into governmental policies by mere legislation until it is a sufficiently large majority to secure the power to do so by the orderly processes of constitutional amendment; and, if it is large enough to do that, then the minority is so small that, while it may bitterly resent the change, it can do no more than gracefully acquiesce. The process of experimental change by one or more states, followed in due course, if the change proves acceptable and desirable, by federal constitutional amendment, thereby becomes a broad highway for reform, by orderly methods, without violence, with a minimum of interference with individual freedom, and without the nation being fastened in a straitjacket of static social and economic philosophy. These things are as true today as they were in 1787, and they were true in 1860.

The keystone of the whole structure lay, of course, in the power of the Supreme Court to keep the majority as represented in the Congress within constitutional limits and to force a reform group on any question to attain the proportions of an amending majority before translating its ideas into governmental policies; and in the ability of the Court to interpret the Constitution as nearly as is possible with mathematical precision and without regard to personal bias on social and economic questions. Whatever may have been the intention of the founding fathers—and John Marshall's dictum is almost indisputable—the Court had been exercising the function for almost three quarters of a century, and any proposal to transfer the seat of the suspensory veto constituted a far-reaching revolutionary movement. No less important than the existence of a Supreme Court, which was independent of a rapidly changing public opinion and whose function it was to restrain temporary majorities, was the principle of free and unlimited discussion of any and all subjects in every part of the Union, that reforms might move forward without too much delay. Any unnatural restraint upon progressive reform in a large group of states, so that changes could not be effected through action of the states themselves or by federal constitutional amendment, would lead to demands by reform advocates that constitutional restraints upon majorities be abolished.   This is exactly what happened between 1830 and 1860.   Both the abolitionists and the devotees of the positive-good argument found the system wholly inadequate.

The antislavery movement, with its roots deeply embedded in Jeffersonian liberalism and the social philosophy of the revolutionary period, received a fresh impulse from the Christian benevolence of the great revival and became a well-organized, skillfully directed moral-reform movement. The proslavery movement, resting completely upon the theory of racial inferiority and biological inequality, emerged from an attitude of apology into a militant defense of the institution as a positive good to both races.   This conflict of ideas called for the widest possible discussion, the most patient inquiry, complete tolerance of opinion, and the humility of disciplined minds and insulated emotions.   It was not, and never should have become, a political question.   It would not have become that had the South shown the slightest disposition to reason.   Instead, it repudiated the most fundamental principles of the American way of life—destroyed the essential element in the democratic system of government, and silenced or exiled its champions of liberalism.   In that, and in its failure to take drastic steps to insure that slavery should be the humane and civilizing institution it was claimed to be, the South committed a serious blunder in strategy.

In the first instance the Southern states had, under the Constitution, complete control over the institution of slavery, including the police powers necessary to sustain it and the exercise of sovereignty necessary to modify or to abolish it. It was futile for them to say that people in other sections had no moral right to discuss the subject.   A moment's reflection on the consequences of a well-organized boycott of slave-produced cotton by the abolitionists of Great Britain and the

United States would have settled that point; and, if not, the arrogance of asking them to catch and return persons to perpetual bondage in a system which was none of their concern would have done so. The Southern states did have within themselves that diversity of social and economic interests which, had it been allowed to function, would have solved the problem. To deny that is to ignore the class distinctions which were at the basis of the two-party system in the South; the fact that many of the most powerful leaders of the abolition movement were Southern exiles; and the stubborn contest to keep abolition literature out of the mails. This self-imposed restraint and the exclusion of all outside influence by the Southern states forced the advocates of the new social philosophy to find other ways and means to modify the *status quo;* and the certain knowledge that, once in control of the power and patronage of the federal government, the antislavery forces would introduce the debate into the South, build up their party there, set non-slaveholder against slaveholder, and bring about the abolition of slavery by the orderly process of state constitutional action, as they had a perfectly ethical and legal right to do, may be set down as the number one reason for secession. Against that probability there was no defense if the Southern states remained in the Union.

The unprecedented action of the Southern states was followed by the equally unprecedented and irregular procedure of the abolitionists in organizing what they intended to be from the first a sectional political party, whose bond of union was and remained hostility to an institution which formed the basis of the social and economic life of fifteen states in another section. Their purpose was to alter the policies of the government with respect to slavery, with a minimum program of excluding slavery from the territories and new slave states from the Union, abolishing slavery in the District of Columbia, prohibiting the interstate slave trade, and repealing the fugitive-slave laws. This purposed circumscription of slavery, with ultimate extinction in view, constituted a revolution in itself, though the elevation of the Republican Party to power was in perfect accord with constitutional form. The uncertain value of slave property in the upper South would quicken the transfer of slaves to the Black Belt, hasten emancipation in food-producing states, like Virginia and Kentucky, make possible emancipation by federal constitutional amendment at an early date—again a perfectly constitutional procedure—and increase the danger of the white population in the lower South being overwhelmed by a slave or free Negro population.

The real significance of the Republican victory, however, lay in its espousal of the higher-law doctrine, aimed directly at the keystone of the governmental structure: the Supreme Court. The Supreme Court had confined itself to an interpretation of the Constitution. It had upheld the fugitive-slave acts. It had opened the territories to slavery. There was no certainty that it would permit the exclusion of slaves from interstate commerce by Congressional action. The abolitionists insisted that the philosophy of the Court be changed; that interpretations of the Constitution be in harmony with the principles of the Declaration of Independence; that judges be appointed who would find the power of Congress adequate to carry out their program. Reorganization of the Court in itself, and still more investing the Declaration with constitutional vitality, would be a circumvention of constitutional safeguards set up for the protection of minorities, a removal of the restraints of the fundamental law, as interpreted by the judiciary, from the will of a numerical majority in a consolidated nation. Carried to the full limits of its possibilities, it would destroy constitutional government. It is purely a matter of speculation how far the party would have gone in this direction, if thwarted in every other effort to reach its objective, because secession and war put other instruments into its hands. That it would have ignored an idea so deep-rooted in abolition doctrines does not seem probable. And so we had the unique situation of the proslavery forces effectively preventing reform by state action by proscribing free discussion. This compelled the antislavery forces to abandon their cause or to move upon slavery through the federal government. Both groups knew that constitutional restraints upon Congressional action would be swept aside by reorganization of the Court. This probability, in turn, caused the South to be apprehensive of the adequacy of existing governmental machinery for the *protection* of slavery. The unique feature of Calhoun's thesis was the idea that constitutional limitations upon the power of the majority were of no value unless authority to enforce the limitations resided in the minority for whose benefits they had been imposed; that if a majority in the nation at large on any question remained in power long enough its philosophy would become the philosophy of the Court, the federal government with its three departments acting harmoniously would arrogate authority to itself, the reserved rights of the states would be invaded, and the minority would be reduced to the feeble status of a suppliant for its rights. There was some precedent for the interposition of state authority as a restraint upon the federal government and in the nature of a defiance or invasion of the particular province of the Supreme Court. Georgia had defied the Court on the Indian question. South Carolina had forced Congress to reduce the tariff. Several northern states had passed legislation in direct contravention of the federal fugitive-slave acts.

Whether these precedents were strong enough to justify the conclusion that they were a recognized part of our constitutional procedure is difficult to determine. It is certain that the secessionists of the slave states believed that in all disputes between a state and the federal government the state, was, in the last analysis, the judge of the extent of its grievances and of the mode and measure of redress; and that the so-called Unionists of the slave states believed that, in a similar case, the burden of proof was upon the federal government, which must, after the state had interposed its sovereignty, either abandon its claim to exercise the powers in dispute or refer the question to the amending power. The two schools of thought embraced the entire South, and the second had strong endorsement in the Northern border states. The Washington Peace Conference episode and the strong antiwar sentiment in the North are conclusive proof of the fact. It is extremely doubtful, therefore, if secession could have been arrested or reunion effected on any basis short of a constitutional amendment embracing the principle of the concurrent majority. It is equally doubtful if, at a time when they were making a practical application of the state-sovereignty thesis, the seven states of the lower South would have sent delegates to a national convention on any basis other than the principle of free consent, with each state, as in 1787, at liberty to ratify or to reject the results of its deliberations.

The Republicans, had they accepted the first of these alternatives, would have surrendered the gains of thirty years' effort to rid the country of slavery, repudiated moral convictions as binding as the tenets of religious faith, shattered their party into factions, and abrogated their right as individuals ever again to seek public office from the electorate. The second alternative required endorsement of the right of secession, equally impossible, and the risk of complete disintegration of the Union or abandonment of fundamental principles of government. No party in the century and a half of the nation's existence has ever ventured to suggest a national convention, each being content to follow the more tedious procedure of Congressional resolution and ratification by the states.

The Republican leaders showed no indication of willingness to make concessions, proceeding on the correct assumption that there was nothing irregular about Lincoln's election and on the incorrect assumption, as the South thought, that there was no cause for excitement or apprehension on the part of anyone. They prevented any sort of compromise in Congress; they exerted pressure to keep the Washington Peace Conference from accomplishing anything in the way of conciliation; and Lincoln himself, without the knowledge of his own cabinet, ordered troops into Fort Pickens five days after his inauguration, with the certain knowledge that war would result. Zebina Eastman, in a private letter after the war, said Lincoln belonged to that group of antislavery men—a not inconsiderable number—who foresaw the impossibility of overthrowing slavery except by war. Be that as it may, his complete silence from the moment of his election until he started for Washington three months later did nothing to ease the tension or allay the apprehensions of peace men in the upper South; and his exposition of extreme consolidation views in his speeches en route caused secession sentiment to sweep that section like a prairie fire.

I firmly believe that the call for troops had little to do with the secession of those states, being the occasion rather than the cause for action. Their love for the Union was greater than their devotion to slavery, but was not equal to the deep-rooted conviction that free government rests upon the consent of the governed. Said the *Charlottesville Review:* "There is a habit of speaking derisively of going to war for *an idea*—an abstraction—something which you cannot see. . . . An idea is exactly the thing that we would fight for. . . . The people who will not fight for ideas will never retain the spirit to fight for anything. Life loses its highest meaning, when opinions become matters of indifference. It is the reproduction of the old fallacy, that it does not matter what a man believes; it is only his acts that are to be looked to. But a false belief necessarily begets wrong actions. A man's belief *is the man*. . . . Therefore, we say, for this *idea* of State honor—for this abstract principle of not bating her just claims upon threat of coercion—we would convulse this Union from centre to circumference."[2]  And the *Missouri Republican:* "Has it come to this that the Union is an entity, distinct from the States which compose it? . . .   Once admitted, and American freedom will soon stand trembling before the Presidential throne.   The States are the true guardians of our freedom and our rights, and when their power is gone, the master at the Federal Capital is the ruler over subject millions—an emperor, elected or self-appointed, as the times determine."[3] And Governor Harris of Tennessee: "Widely as we may differ with some of our sister Southern States as to the wisdom of their policy . . . the question at last, is one which each member of the Confederacy must determine for itself; and any attempt upon the part of the others to hold, by means of military force, an unwilling sovereignty as a member of a common Union, must inevitably lead to the worst form of internecine war, and if successful, result in the establishment of a new and totally different government from the one established by the Constitution—a Constitutional Union being a Union of Consent and not of force, of peace, and not of blood—composed of sovereignties, free, and politically equal.   But the new and coercive government, while it would 'derive its powers' to govern a portion of the states 'from the consent of the governed,' would derive the power by which it governed the remainder from the cannon and the sword, and not from their consent—a Union, not of equals, but of the victors and the vanquished, pinned together by the bayonet and congealed in blood."[4]

One of the most interesting aspects of the entire movement was the readiness of the Southern people to applaud

[2] *The Review* (Charlottesville, Va.), January 25, 1861, in *ibid.,* p. 415.

[3] *Daily Missouri Republican,* April 19, 1861, in *ibid.,* pp. 500–501.

[4] Governor Isham G. Harris to the Legislature of Tennessee, January 7, 1861, in *The Daily True Delta* (New Orleans), January 13, 1861.

threats of disunion by their statesmen over a long period of years and their reluctance finally to take the step. Whenever the prevailing philosophy of Negro inferiority, pressure politics, and their adroitness as politicians seemed inadequate to win their point on a particular question, Southerners had resorted to threats of disunion to strengthen their position. Irrespective of whether the threat to dissolve the Union was the deciding factor in the admission of Missouri, the eviction of the Indians, the modification of the tariff, the failure to abolish slavery in the District, and the ban on antislavery petitions, the fact that every time the threat had been made the South had emerged victorious and that on each new occasion the cry of disunion was louder and more ominous must have increased their faith in its efficacy. There was more than a modicum of truth in Birney's prediction in 1836: "After achieving so much by a process so simple, why should not the South persist in it when striving for further conquests? No other course ought to be expected from her, till this has failed. And it is not at all improbable, that she will persist, till she almost persuades herself that she is serious in her menace to dissolve the Union. She may in her eagerness, even approach so near the verge of dissolution, that the earth may give way under her feet and she be dashed in ruins in the gulf below."[5]

The poor reception given to the League of United Southerners; the repudiation of secession in resistance to the compromise measures of 1850; the refusal to join in a Southern conference in 1859; the maintenance of their political identity by the Whigs in 1860; and the vehemence with which they denounced the Breckinridge Democrats as secessionists per se—all these things indicate a deep-seated aversion to disunion. However much men might concede the right of secession, they were unwilling to be placed in a position where secession would be necessary to save their self-respect.

[5] *Birney–Elmore Correspondence*, p. 42.

The Alabama Democracy, under the leadership of William L. Yancey, led the way in the political contest of 1860 by pledging the state to secession in event of a Republican victory. As the campaign progressed, Southern Breckinridge Democrats, in Congress and out, vied with one another in placing emphasis upon the necessity for secession if Lincoln should be elected. They thundered from every rostrum the notion that quick and emphatic unity in support of a party pledged to disrupt the Union if Lincoln should be elected would cause the Northern people to hesitate in their mad rush to the antislavery standard, and would bring about his defeat. Their opponents, the old Whigs, now Constitutional Unionists, no less faithful to Southern rights, insisted that a heavy vote for Breckinridge would embolden the advocates of disunion and a light vote would cause them to hesitate before inaugurating extreme measures. Every staunch defender of Southern rights had compromised his freedom of action by committing himself in advance to a program of action in an event before the event took place. It was a deathblow to deliberation. It may well have been the determining factor in the secession movement.

Finally, there was the question of reunion at some future date on a more permanent and enduring basis than before. The great sorrow of men like Alexander Stephens and Clement Vallandigham was that secession had split the forces fighting against concentration of power in the central government. Each group, in its own section, waged a bitter campaign against the exercise of arbitrary power by the Lincoln and Davis governments. The Davis party may be regarded as the group who believed permanent separation desirable and inevitable and every action justified that would promote a military victory and the permanency of the Confederacy. The opposition included both the Yancey secessionists and the Stephens state-rights men who had counseled against immediate secession. The latter had been influential in adopting the Constitution of the United States with minor alterations. The need of quick action in establishing the new government, the fact that their quarrel was not with the Constitution but the North's interpretation of it, the degree to which it would facilitate negotiation of foreign treaties, and the minimum of readjustment it would require in the lives of the people—all these were in part responsible for the decision. But one cannot ignore the strong probability that many men hoped for a not-too-long-delayed reunion and knew that few changes in the system of government enhanced its possibility.

Truth must, therefore, bear witness to the fact that men created a new nation on the professed principle of liberty and equality for all men while clinging tenaciously to a system of human bondage; that the power and influence of the system grew so strong as to threaten the liberties of all men; and that finally a civil war which shook the nation to its foundations was required to abolish it. It must record that men who lived under its baneful influence became so enraptured by its superlative qualities as a system of racial adjustment and cultural advancement that they repudiated the only real specific of human progress ever discovered—the spirit of free inquiry—and, in the end, were willing to plunge a great people into internecine strife, wrench apart the fraternal affection of millions of people, and destroy the rich spiritual heritage of their posterity, if need be, to preserve it. It must place particular emphasis upon the fact that men who might have been willing to embark upon an unprecedented experiment in social and economic readjustment held still more precious than life itself the right of men to order their own lives and to determine the limits of the powers of their own government. And it must lead us, in the end, to the melancholy reflection that the political machinery of a great people broke down completely in the crisis and gave passion and crime the mastery over sober counsel, equity, and justice.

# INDEX

# ANN ARBOR PAPERBACKS

*reissues of works of enduring merit*

*The University of Michigan Press  /  Ann Arbor*